CROWOOD SPORTS GUIDES
TRIATHLON
SKILLS • TECHNIQUES • TACTICS

CROWOOD SPORTS GUIDES
TRIATHLON
SKILLS • TECHNIQUES • TACTICS

Steve Trew

THE CROWOOD PRESS

First published in 2010 by
The Crowood Press Ltd
Ramsbury, Marlborough
Wiltshire SN8 2HR

www.crowood.com

British Library Cataloguing-in-Publication Data
A catalogue record for this book is available from the British Library.

ISBN 978 1 84797 170 8

Dedication
For Marilyn and for Shane, who changed my life even more than triathlon.

Acknowledgements
My thanks to Nigel Farrow for his inspiring photography, and to athletes Emma Dearsley and
Toby Radcliffe for their patience and humour throughout all the sequence shots.
My thanks also to the athletes with whom I have worked over the years. You have all
been inspirations.

Disclaimer
Please note that the author and the publisher of this book are not responsible or liable, in any
manner whatsoever, for any damage, injury, or adverse outcome of any kind that may result from
practising, or applying, the techniques and methods and/or following the instructions described in
this publication. Since the exercises and other physical activities described in this book may be too
strenuous in nature for some readers to engage in safely, it is essential that a doctor is consulted
before undertaking such exercises and activities

Typeset by Bookcraft Ltd, Stroud, Gloucestershire
Printed and bound in India by Replika Press

CONTENTS

PREFACE

Triathlon is a sport that has caught the public's imagination; perhaps following on from the marathon boom, triathlon is seen as the all-round sport that will not only keep you fit and active but also promote an active and balanced lifestyle.

This book advises on the basic skills and techniques of the three disciplines which comprise triathlon, and provides help on balancing the training required in a multi-discipline sport. An analysis of swimming, cycling and running, along with the fourth discipline, the transition, and the particular training required to be able to deal with that, is set alongside sequence photographs that explain the appropriate techniques.

There is also advice on preparation for and analysis of racing, as well as tapering, nutrition and achieving that essential positive mental attitude.

PART I
INTRODUCTION TO TRIATHLON

CHAPTER I

THE SPORT: HISTORY AND DISCIPLINES

Triathlon is a multi-discipline sport comprising swimming, cycling and running. These disciplines are normally undertaken one immediately after the other with no break in between. The changeover between the disciplines is called the transition.

Triathlon History

Popular myth has it that the sport of triathlon began in Hawaii, but this is not true: triathlon's roots can be traced back to sunny, southern California in 1974, at Mission Bay in San Diego. Jack Johnstone and Don Shanahan organized this triathlon, taking over and moving on from a swim-and-run biathlon staged the previous year. Jack Johnstone added a bike discipline, and the sport of triathlon was born. However, triathlon had very little initial impact. Very slowly more triathlons were organized in and around the San Diego area and some were held a little further afield, though mainly still in southern California. There was no overall organization or structure at this time and both the distances of the three disciplines and the overall length of events differed widely. Often the distances would reflect the strengths and weaknesses of the race organizers and their experience, particularly if they intended taking part in their own event. There were individual races, relays, and events with two or more separate distances in some or all of the disciplines.

Fast transitions are an integral part of triathlon. © Nigel Farrow

One man who did take part in that first ever triathlon in Mission Bay was a certain John Collins, and it is perhaps thanks to him that triathlon has established its current popularity. John Collins was a naval captain at the time he took part in the event; he was later promoted to commander. Just three years after the Mission Bay triathlon, Captain Collins was a competitor in the relay running event around Hawaii. After this event, in discussion with other athletes and competitors, not only runners, John Collins came up with a proposal that was to popularize triathlon. In 1977 there were three endurance events on the island of Oahu; the Waikiki rough water swim of 2.4 miles (3km), a two-day cycle event around the island of 112 miles (180km), and the Honolulu marathon of 26.2 miles (42km). In 1978 on 18 February, the dream became a reality and Gordon Haller (USA) won the first ever 'Ironman' event in 11 hours 46 minutes. Of the 15 athletes who started the event, 12 finished. Television coverage followed in 1980 and the Ironman became too big for Oahu and was moved to the 'big' island of Hawaii.

Triathlon achieved real fame and even notoriety in 1982. Triathlete Julie Moss was leading the women's event when, within sight of the finish line, she collapsed and began to crawl towards and over the finish line, only for Kathleen McCartney to run past her. The TV and general media coverage captured the imagination of all watching, and guaranteed continued interest from the general public, who perceived this new sport as something outside the normal run of things.

From its early beginnings in California and Hawaii, triathlon started to gain acceptance as a sport in its own right in Europe in 1982. Scott Tinley, a leading US triathlete had been commissioned by the International Management Group (IMG) to organize a triathlon in the principality of Monaco. However, Princess Grace of Monaco (formerly Hollywood film star Grace Kelly) was killed in a car crash and the race had to be abandoned. As all the planning had been done, the race was moved to Nice, France, and a number of the top Americans raced including Mark Allen who went on to win the inaugural

Simon Whitfield of Canada, the first Olympic male gold medalist for triathlon, in Sydney 2000.
© Nigel Farrow

ITU World Championships in 1989 and many Hawaii Ironman Championships.

Dagenham newsagent Aleck Hunter was the man who brought triathlon to Great Britain. Aleck had raced in that first Nice event and was captivated by the sheer professionalism and discipline of the American athletes in particular. Together with Olympic pentathlete Mike Ellis, and endurance cycling record holder Dick Poole, Aleck formed the British Triathlon Association (BTA) in 1983 over a drink in a Hammersmith pub.

In these early days, organization of triathlon tended to be fragmented and a little haphazard, and it was not until 1989, the year of the first Triathlon World Championships in Avignon, France, that the world organizing body, the International Triathlon Union (ITU) was founded. The BTA eventually became the British Triathlon Federation (BTF). In a very short time, triathlon was accepted into the Olympic Games and made its debut in Sydney 2000. Australia has become one of the world's leading lights in triathlon and it was entirely appropriate that its Olympic debut was here. The distances of this first Olympic triathlon were 1500m swim, 40k

cycle and 10k run. These distances had been accepted as the standard distances for a number of years since that first world championship, and were taken from existing events on the Olympic programme in the separate sports of swimming, cycling and running. The Commonwealth Games followed in Manchester, England in 2002; the 2004 Olympic Games in Athens, Greece; 2006 Commonwealth Games in Melbourne, Australia and then the 2008 Olympic Games in Beijing, China.

World championships in triathlon have been held every year since 1989 as have continental championships including European championships.

The Disciplines

The three disciplines of triathlon are swimming, cycling and running. However, the nature of the sport – with no time gap between disciplines – has created a fourth discipline: the transition, or changeover between events.

Many people accept that it is this continuous nature and fast change that have made triathlon unique. There are, of

course, many other multi-discipline sports: the decathlon and heptathlon in track and field, the modern pentathlon mix of swimming and running, fencing, shooting and riding. But these events are not non-stop and continuous; triathlon is. In the early days in Great Britain, swimming was sometimes replaced by canoeing, and still today there are variations on the triathlon theme. One popular substitute is indoor rowing on a fixed machine such as the Concept 2. However the swim–cycle–run format is now accepted as triathlon proper, although local conditions may occasionally mean that the order may differ, or one discipline may be split.

Emma Snowshill of Australia and Vanessa Fernandez of Portugal, gold and silver medal winners in the Beijing Olympic triathlon. © *Nigel Farrow*

Everything about triathlon is exciting! © *Nigel Farrow*

CHAPTER 2

GETTING STARTED: FACILITIES AND EQUIPMENT

What do we need in the way of facilities – a place to train—for triathlon? Ideally, the same facilities that are needed for our three discipline sports: swimming, cycling and running

Swimming

For swimming, a swimming pool is of course essential and additionally, access to a safe open water venue is a big advantage. Swimming pools come in all shapes and sizes, perhaps the most common are the standard 25-metre long pool although some areas still have the older 33.3-metre pool. (There still some 25-yard pools in existence, and many of the older 33.3-metre pools are actually $36^2/_3$ yards, because the distances competed in Great Britain were 110 yards rather than 100m.) There are 50-metre pools, but these are still few and far between. There is almost always public swimming in local authority pools but this can sometimes be crowded and unpleasant for novice swimmers. However, most enlightened authorities now have time set aside, often in the early mornings, for serious swimmers who perhaps don't want to belong to a swimming club. At these times, some (perhaps all) of the pool will be sectioned or laned off, and swimmers will be able to swim up and down the lane. Most pools will also have designated slow, medium and fast lanes or recreational, semi-serious and serious swimmer lanes so that people are able to choose the most appropriate standard for them. However, it is far better to be able

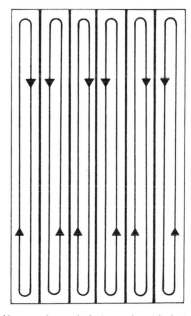

Alternate lanes clockwise and anticlockwise to avoid unnecessary collisions

Pool layout and lane patterns.

to swim under guidance, particularly for novice swimmers. Swimming is all about technique, and without a good technique, progress will be minimal. Most swimming clubs now have a 'masters' section for swimmers (normally) over the age of twenty years, some even have a fitness or triathlon section to cater for adults. The importance of the help of a qualified teacher or coach cannot be over-emphasized, and improvement in technique can

be fast. You will normally be told to swim in a clockwise or anticlockwise direction for safety reasons to avoid collisions. Alternate lanes will swim in alternate directions to avoid the possibility of arms clashing as they recover over the water.

Access to a safe, open water venue is a huge advantage for the triathlete intending to race in open water events. It is essential that the venue is safe, that the water quality is good and that there is always some form of safety and rescue on hand. Triathletes and swimmers should *never* swim alone or unsupervised. Lakes are normally safer than rivers or the sea; currents and tides can be deceptive and dangerous.

Kit and Equipment for Swimming

While some triathletes prefer to wear an all-in-one 'trisuit' for competitions, for training swimming trunks or costume are the essentials, but there are also the almost-essentials and a variety of other equipment that will help in training.

Foremost of these are swimming goggles. Swimming goggles have only really been in existence for twenty years or so and prior to this, weeping eyes during and after swimming training sessions were commonplace amongst swimmers. Goggles protect the eyes from chemicals and infection and also greatly assist sighting, looking at their own or other swimmers' techniques under water.

Swimming caps or hats will keep long hair out of a swimmer's eyes and will also help in maintaining body heat, particularly

Many triathletes prefer to wear a trisuit. © *Nigel Farrow*

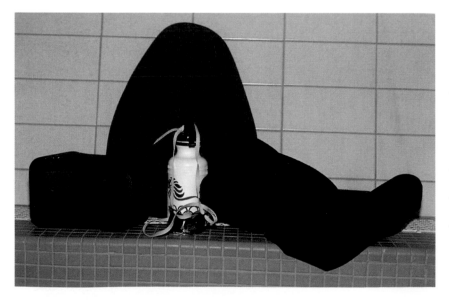

The swimmer's kit.

in open water swims (one-third of body heat is lost through the head). Neoprene or insulated hats are also a great advantage in open water swimming when the temperature is low.

Kickboards and pull buoys are used to isolate and focus on the leg action and arm action. However, overuse of these can be detrimental. Good kick action is essential to make progress in swimming, even though it is predominantly an upper body activity; new triathletes will often try to 'short-cut' their swimming deficiencies by too much use of the pull buoy that will lift their body position artificially. Similarly, too much use of kickboards can make the lower back sore and make the kicking process artificial.

Fins (often wrongly called flippers) are extremely useful, particularly when starting to learn new drills and techniques, as they remove the necessity of having to kick hard to maintain a good, flat body position. They are also very useful for kick practice but kicking work should also take place without the use of fins. Short, specialist swim fins are essential. The long, underwater and snorkelling fins can slow down the kick, giving a false sense of ability; they also put pressure on ankles and feet when kicking hard.

A water bottle is essential for all the disciplines, not only swimming. Particularly in swimming, the effects of not drinking enough, early enough, and possible dehydration can easily be underrated.

Rubber tubing can be used around the ankles to isolate the legs and force the swimmer to focus on pulling. They quickly give an insight into how important good kicking is for balance and position.

A wetsuit is essential for open water swimming in Great Britain. A specialist swimming wetsuit is advisable and recommended. Diving, surfing and canoeing wetsuits are often too inflexible and are unsuitable. The neoprene rubber of the wetsuit comes in different thicknesses (often 3mm and 5mm) and you should take advice on what is best for you.

Wetsuits are essential when the water is cold. © Nigel Farrow

Cycling

Cycling can be practised wherever there are roads. However, traffic on roads is inherently dangerous and care must always be taken when deciding where to ride. This is particularly important when in a new area, perhaps arriving early at a race venue. (Greg Welch, Australian Triathlon world champion was stopped when found cycling along the motorway when in Manchester for the 1993 World Championships.) Ideally, stay away from main and busy roads; also be wary in country lanes where traffic may not anticipate one or more cyclists coming around a corner. Above all, exercise caution! Hills are a necessary and welcome evil. If you don't ride hills in training, then you won't ride hills well in races.

Getting off the roads and mountain biking in safe surroundings is recommended, but you will need caution again if you are not an experienced mountain bike rider: the chance of falls and accidents can be higher.

Highly recommended is a turbo trainer (sometimes called a 'wind trainer' or 'wind load simulator'). A turbo trainer is a floor-based metal frame with a roller at the back. You set your bike on this with the rear wheel on the roller. Pressure can be adjusted for the roller and wheel. The front wheel is sometimes still attached to the bike, sometimes removed, and the front forks safely fixed. You are ready to train safely on the cycle indoors. One advantage of this is that there can be no distractions when doing a quality, interval-based training session. The turbo trainer is a valuable tool that will help training immensely.

Cycling Equipment and Clothing

You will need a bike that must fit you perfectly. Your mechanical efficiency and aerodynamics position will depend on this. You also need to be comfortable. The main components and equipment on a bike are: frame, wheels and tyres, freewheel, chain, brakes, headset, handlebars and stem, gears, chainwheel and bottom bracket, pedals.

Although bike size is important, it is not the be-all and end-all as there are a number of adjustments that can be made. Sizing and position adjustments can only be guidelines, and if you do need to make changes, make them gradually and in easy stages of a maximum half-centimetre each time. The adjustments that can be easily made for height and for reach are: saddle height, saddle front and rear position, handlebar height, and handlebar forward and back position (stem length).

The most important piece of clothing is not shoes, shorts or jersey, but a crash-hat. You have to wear a crash-hat to be allowed to compete; you can be disqualified if you are seen riding at a race without one. Wearing a crash-hat may save your life; it did mine.

Cycle shorts have a chamois or padded insert in the crotch area to make you comfortable when sitting on a saddle for a long time. A cycle jersey has two or three pockets at the back to allow you to carry food and emergency repair articles. Make sure that you always have a water bottle, puncture repair outfit and/or spare inner tube, and a mobile phone. Your bike

Riding up hills is a necessary evil. © Nigel Farrow

Olympic triathlete Hollie Avil on the turbo trainer. © Nigel Farrow

should have a water bottle carrier and a pump attached to the frame. Wearing cycle mitts (gloves) will stop your hands rubbing on the handlebars.

Running

You can run anywhere. However, as with cycling it can be pleasant to choose a quiet route away from main roads. Running on grass can often be easier on the legs because of the softer surfaces. The down-side of a grass surface is that it may not always be level so it is important to watch where you are running. It is extremely useful to have access to a 400-metre running track so that periodically you can check and monitor your training times. Most running tracks are now all-weather surfaces with eight lanes. If you choose to run in any lane except lane one (and some tracks insist on this to save wear and tear on the inside lane), you will run further than 400m each time and your times will demonstrate that.

Running Clothing

The most important item of running clothing and equipment is a good pair of shoes. With these, you are more likely to avoid injury. However, there is no one correct type of running shoe and each individual will need ones that suit them. There is a great deal of choice: straight, slightly curved and curved; board-lasted (normally the heavier training shoes) and slip-lasted (normally the lighter racing shoes), or a combination of both with the board-lasting from heel to mid-foot. Care must be taken when changing to a new, different pair of shoes as there can be a significant difference in foot plant with a new shoe. It is also helpful to seek advice as to whether you are a pronator (where the ankle pushes inwards on foot plant), a neutral runner (straight on foot plant), or supinator (where the ankle pushes outwards on foot plant). The majority of runners are pronators or neutral type runners. Most good specialist running shops will give this advice.

Running shorts and vests should be comfortable and light; if you are new to running, it is worth knowing that many a runner suffers from sore nipples when their vest rubs on the chest. Applying Vaseline will stop this. Lace locks rather than laces will save a few seconds in the transition area when changing from cycling to running shoes. Hats, sunglasses, woolly hats and running tights are also useful for changes in weather.

Finally, heart rate monitors (which do what they say, monitor your heart rate) are useful tools to check how hard you are training. These can be used for all three disciplines including swimming, although male swimmers may want to wear a trisuit rather than swimming trunks to keep the heart rate monitor in place on the chest.

Running can be done anywhere. © *Nigel Farrow*

Racing in a pack can still be fun. © *Nigel Farrow*

CHAPTER 3

THE TRIATHLON FAMILY

Triathlon is swim, bike and run. However, there are other combinations that are part of the triathlon family and are governed by national and the international bodies.

Duathlon

Duathlon used to be called biathlon and is like triathlon for non-swimmers; you run, then you bike and then you run again. Biathlon became duathlon to avoid confusion with the winter sport of the same name that incorporates cross-country skiing and rifle shooting. Duathlon has a lower profile than triathlon and is not (yet) an Olympic sport. The ITU, triathlon's governing body, runs a World Championship for both elite and age group athletes over a short distance of 10k run, 40k cycle and 5k run; and a long distance of 10k, 60k, 10k. However, perhaps more so than in triathlon, duathlon competition distances can vary. Athletes who want to run and cycle even further can enter the Powerman events, a world series of events based around the original Power(wo)man Zofingen race which has a 10k first run, 150k bike and 30k second run. Not all the events are this long but they have to be a minimum of 10k:60k:10k to be part of the long distance series.

Aquathon

The aquathon is a swim–run event. Unlike a duathlon that traditionally has three stages (run, bike, run) an aquathon often has just two: swim and run. The swim usually, but not always, precedes the run. Aquathons take place all year round and distances range from as short as a 500m pool swim and a 5k run up to 2000m open water swims and 10k runs. The ITU organizes its aquathon World Championships as a run–swim–run event with the second run normally half the distance of the first, although sometimes it is a 2.5k run, 1k swim, 2.5k run.

Another variation of the sport, and run under the pentathlon governing body, is biathle. This is also a run–swim–run combination and has a series of events around the world and a World Championship.

There is also aquabike wherein you swim and then bike, but the discipline has no formal status and these are often races put on as part of an overall triathlon-based competition weekend where the organizer is trying to offer variety.

Winter Triathlon

Winter triathlon is yet another variant. It consists of running, mountain biking, and cross-country skiing. The International Triathlon Union also holds World Championships for this. Usually, the events in winter triathlon are all held on snow, often on cross-country ski trails. Courses tend to be multiple laps for each leg with separate courses for the run, mountain bike and ski portions. The most common distances for races are 5–8km for the run, 8–12km for the mountain bike, and 6–10km for the ski discipline. On the run, competitors wear running shoes with heavily indented treads or, occasionally, cross-country running spikes. All kinds of mountain bike are permitted and will usually have very wide tyres to maximize grip. Unlike road triathlons, the tyre pressure will be low, also to help grip the snow better. The cross-country ski leg can be undertaken with either the classical diagonal stride or the freestyle/skating option. The freestyle/skating style is generally chosen.

Swimming, an essential skill. © Nigel Farrow

Pure open water swimming does not allow wetsuits. © *Nigel Farrow*

Individual Disciplines

Along with the multi-discipline variants, it is also important to recognize the contribu-tory sports of swimming, cycling and run-ning. Most triathletes will also compete in at least one of the single disciplines, which is often initially their 'background' sport, but as they look to gain more experience, the likelihood is that they will enter the other individual discipline competitions.

Swimming

Although swimming is often perceived as a young person's sport, there is a thriving Masters section of older swimmers in Great Britain and throughout the world with their own national, international and world championships. Many swimming clubs now have active Masters sections and this will enable you to train and to race. Competition ages are similar to those in triathlon, with five-year age bands; this ensures that you will compete against similar age and standard competi-tors. The natural move for triathletes is to take part (or at least to train) in open water swimming events. These are organ-ized by the British Long Distance Swim-ming Association (BLDSA) and can range in length from as little as 500m up to and

Elite triathletes are allowed to draft just as in road racing. © *Nigel Farrow*

beyond the famous cross channel swims between England and France of over 20 miles (32km). Wetsuits are not permitted in BLDSA-organized swimming events.

Cycling

The main two options for cycling are road racing and time trialling. Road racing is a massed-start activity with cyclists starting together in a bunch. It is probably more relevant to elite triathlon than age group races, although if you are able to race, it gives a great opportunity for bike handling and learning the skills of bike control.

Time trialling occurs when riders start one after another at a fixed time gap, which is normally – but not always – a minute. It is an individual event with riders often attempting to race against themselves by beating previous recorded times as well as racing against the other competitors in the field. There are many local, club-organized events where new riders are welcome to turn up, perhaps 30 minutes before the event starts, pay a modest entry fee of one or two pounds and race. Common club trial distances are 10 and 25 miles (16 and 40km), but can also be 50 and 100 miles (80 and 160km).

Running

This discipline gives the option of track, road and cross-country running. While it may seem that road or cross-country running are more relevant to triathlon, it is also important to work on speed and triathletes can learn a lot by entering an open event in a middle distance or longer distance race of between as short as 800m or as long as 10,000m.

With all three of the individual sports, it is helpful to be a member of a club. That way you can take advantage of local and inside knowledge, find training partners and learn a little about the culture of the sport.

Running off-road is a pleasant alternative. © *Nigel Farrow*

Track training for running is a great help to building speed. © *Nigel Farrow*

CHAPTER 4

COACHING AND TEACHING TRIATHLON

Communication

Coaching triathlon is more than three times as complicated as coaching an individual sport: not only is it three times the coaching, it is also the acknowledgement by the coach of the effect that each discipline has on each of the others.

The coach has to be a teacher, a personal trainer, a motivator and inspirer and also a hard taskmaster. Coaches can also be managers, friends, counsellors and sports scientists. The term 'Jack of all trades' could have been invented for coaching.

Coaching is all about communication. Knowledge of a sport and its technique is not enough to make an effective coach unless the coach's communication skills are excellent. The coach's communication is a mixture of many things, including:

- voice projection and speech
- being in the correct place to coach
- the ability to demonstrate (not necessarily personally but to be able to use a demonstrator)
- clear instruction
- effective body language
- the ability to create mental pictures.

We all think largely in pictures, being able to paint those pictures in the triathlete's mind can be invaluable.

However the coach should not take on the responsibility of imparting all information, but should give athletes the responsibility of discovering aspects of all three disciplines for themselves. Coaches must be aware of the different demands of working:

- with different numbers: individuals, small and large groups
- with athletes from different age groups
- with athletes of differing cultural and national backgrounds.

Coaching in three disciplines will also add a further dimension to the challenges of coaching triathlon. The swimming environment means that the athletes cannot hear or see anything while they are training, so working on technique points will necessitate stopping and restarting the swimmers. The cycling setting is often on the open road with all its inherent dangers; it may be better to hold some coaching and teaching session for cycling on a closed cycle track or on the turbo trainers.

Running may be the easiest discipline to coach when the athletes are on a circuit, either a formal running track or perhaps a training circuit in the woods or on a hill, but there will also be the necessity for longer runs where the coach might accompany them on a bicycle. There are practical limitations in all triathlon disciplines and part of the challenge of coaching the sport is overcoming and using these limitations.

It is important that athletes are involved in the learning and coaching process. Passive acceptance of the coach's words will not lead to improvement unless there is an understanding of why and how changes should be put into place. Looking for reactions from athletes, demonstrating and asking athletes to demonstrate, the question and answer process, and asking for feedback after instruction and practice will all help to ensure better coaching and teaching. Setting targets and challenges are also effective weapons in the coach's

Coach Dan Salcedo gives last minute instructions to Will Clarke of Great Britain.
© Nigel Farrow

armoury. Athletes will respond better if they have something to aim at and believe that appropriate practice of a particular aspect of technique will give better results. Sometimes athletes will say that training is 'boring'. If this happens frequently, the coach should question their own coaching methods. Training has the potential to be boring, but with a well-designed programme with clear instructions and reasons for a particular training phase, that potential should be overcome.

Every coach will have their own way of coaching and their experience of coaching will have taught them what methods work well with particular athletes. For their part, athletes will choose and leave coaches for a variety of reasons; there is no one way of coaching that is correct and different personalities can make a difference to that choice. It is important (for young coaches especially) to realize that not all coach–athlete relationships will be smooth and permanent. It is also important to realize that there is nothing wrong with this. Athletes will leave particular coaches, other athletes will be attracted to that coach. It is an open and never-ending process and the realization of that makes it far easier for athletes to cooperate with coaches.

The Great Britain squad used to be based in Stellenbosch, South Africa for a nine-week period from January to March each year. The author shared coaching duties with two outstanding coaches, Bill Black and Chris Jones. While the athletes would be on camp for all or most of the time, we coaches would switch every three weeks with a couple of days' change-over period. It was absolutely essential that our teamwork was beyond reproach and that we were able to deal with athletes whom we personally coached, who were coached by another one of us, or whose coach was not present on the camp. We were also faced with situations where athletes who had been coached by one of us had then decided to move to a different member of our triumvirate! Fortunately we had the highest regard for each other and appreciated that dealing with personalities and situations like this was an inescapable part of coaching at the top level, particu-larly in an intense training camp environment.

Whole-Part-Whole and the Big Mac Attack

Every coach will have favourite methods of coaching and imparting information: many are shared, some are individual. Two that seem to work well are the 'whole-part-whole' method, and the 'Big Mac attack' methods. The whole-part-whole is almost self-explanatory: a technique or skill is demonstrated and practised as one, then broken down into its parts, and finally practised again as a whole. This is a well known and frequently used technique of coaching.

As everybody is aware, the Big Mac is a meat burger in between two halves of a bread bun, and this is the structure of the 'attack'. The Big Mac attack starts softly with the top bread: the coach says something like, 'Generally your stroke is looking good!' which makes the athlete happy. Then comes the meat, the important part: the coach says, 'But I think we could make it even better by just focusing on … (the coaching or teaching point)'. Then comes the bottom bread, 'But overall, you're doing pretty well!'

The athlete is left satisfied with progress but with a willingness to work on the single aspect of technique mentioned, in order to improve even further.

In whatever form it takes, communication is the single most important part of successful coaching.

Coaching Strategy and Development of Coaching

The British Triathlon Federation is the overall governing body for triathlon in Great Britain. The BTF has worked closely with Sports Coach UK and with the world governing body for triathlon, the International Triathlon Union (ITU), to promote coaching and coach education. The BTF coaching strategy is acknowledged as one of the best in the world.

The submission by the British Triathlon Federation was of an exceptional standard and they can certainly be regarded among the leaders in triathlon coach education worldwide. ITU is proud to endorse all the existing levels of certification offered by this federation and with confidence will recommend these excellent programmes to coaches around the globe.

Libby Burrell, ITU Sport Development Director

I am obliged to Mr Paul Moss of the BTF for the information which concludes this chapter.

The infrastructure of coaching and coach education is based on the following principles:

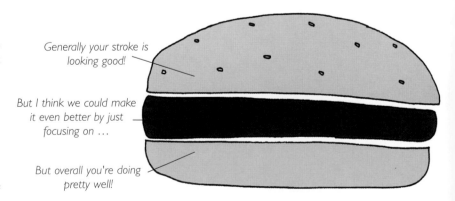

Generally your stroke is looking good!

But I think we could make it even better by just focusing on …

But overall you're doing pretty well!

The Big Mac attack.

Building Performance Pathways: producing skilled quality coaches operating at all stages of development

Building Profile: more quality coaches coaching children and adults at all stages of participant development pathway model, maintaining international endorsement status and recognition as having one of the best triathlon coach education systems in the world

Building Participation: increasing numbers of qualified coaches at a local level will provide more opportunities for coached sessions within clubs and schools, to prepare individuals to achieve their personal triathlon challenges

Business Operations: develop quality systems and databases, instil best practice and provide a high quality level of service to all coaches and members of the home nations.

The BTF coaching qualifications are: introductory level one, leading on to levels two, three and four, with level five as High Performance coach. Within this structure are the provisions of the key benefits delivered by quality coaching to children, their parents, adult participants and communities:

- welcome children and adults into the sport of triathlon
- make triathlon an enjoyable, positive experience for everyone
- build fundamental skills in participants
- improve triathlon skills and techniques
- develop fair play, ethical practice, discipline and respect
- enhance physical fitness and positive lifestyles
- guide children and athletes through the steps to improved performance
- place a high value on the development of the whole person
- keep children and athletes safe in the sport
- integrate the best of coaching and scientific practice into their work
- provide opportunities for wider social learning
- promote leadership and decision-making.

It is also recognized that whilst coaching can be, and usually is, highly beneficial, inappropriate coaching can be at best ineffective, and at worst negative. Central to the BFT coaching plan will be improvement of the quality of coaching at all levels, including coaching of and for disabled tri athletes. As well as developing their ability to guide improvement in technical, tactical and physical domains, coaches have a key role in developing key social, personal and lifestyle capacities. Increasingly, coaches must develop their own people skills to maximize their effectiveness and the quality of their interaction with triathletes.

Guiding Principles of the UK Coaching Strategy

The coaching strategy is guided by the following principles.

- The needs of children, athletes and disabled people are central to the development of the sport. Athlete-centred coaching is a core principle of the UK Coaching Model for Triathlon.
- Triathlon should be welcoming and inclusive of children and participants of all backgrounds. Coaching has a key role to play in embracing diversity and promoting inclusion for all groups especially disabled people, vulnerable adults and children, women and girls, black and minority ethnic groups, older people, gay, lesbian and bisexual participants and lower socio-economic classes.
- Children have a right to be safe, nurtured, healthy, active and happy in triathlon, while enjoying the thrill of physical activity, the challenges of making progress and the satisfaction of achievement. Children and athletes should be supported to take responsibility for their own actions and to deal positively with the emotional demands of involvement in triathlon.
- Triathlon experiences are built most strongly from personal motivation, family, coach, peer, club and school

support. Hence, effective and quality assured coaching operating at local, club and school level is of the highest priority.

- Parents have a key role in encouraging and supporting their children's involvement in sport.
- Coaches are central to increasing and sustaining participation in triathlon sport; achieving success; enhancing the health and quality of life of individuals and communities through athlete-centred coaching.
- While the UK Coaching Framework for Triathlon provides a UK-wide framework for the development of coaching, the personal ownership by coaches of their own development is a core underpinning principle. Valuing and empowering coaches will be a central feature of the Plan.
- The practice of coaching should be underpinned by both 'art' and 'science', recognizing the need for an appropriate mix between the practical experience and expertise of the coach and the application of relevant methodological and scientific principles.

The coach education workforce (Coach Educators, Assessors, Verifiers and Mentors) acts as an important support system in the development of quality coaches.

To help facilitate British Triathlon's overall vision by creating and implementing a cohesive ethical and inclusive world-leading coaching system, whereby skilled triathlon coaches support children and athletes at all stages of their development, which is number one in the world by 2013, the BTF Coaching Strategy will attempt to deliver the following results for triathlon in the UK:

- **Enhance the quality of coaching at all stages of the participant pathway** measured through observable coaching behaviours and participant outcomes including technical, tactical, mental, physical skills as well as personal and social development
- Match the demand for coaching provision from children and adult

participants with a supply of suitably qualified coaches at each stage of the pathway measured by the supply of quality coaching hours to meet the demand at each pathway stage; the availability of suitably qualified coaches as part of sport specific workforce development plans

- **Ensure that coaches' profiles reflect the profiles of participation at all stages of the participation model for triathlon, leading to:**
  - **Increased and sustained participation in triathlon** measured by recruitment, retention and frequency of participation at each stage of the pathway
  - **Improved performances at all stages of the participant pathway model** measured by internationally bench-marked performances at each competitive pathway phase and on a regional, home country and UK-wide basis

  Underpinned by:
  - Clear career structures for coaches as part of a professionally regulated vocation, recognizing volunteer, part-time and full-time roles measured against a clear model of long-term coach development
  - **A Cohesive and World-leading Coaching System** bench-marked against international best practice using the dimensions of the proposed Coaching Scorecard.

It is highly recommended that new triathletes should seek advice from the BTF with regard to coaching and coaches. The BTF can be contacted on info@britishtriathlon.org

Great coaching leads to great performance. © *Nigel Farrow*

CHAPTER 5

TRIATHLON FOR HEALTH

Strength, Endurance and Flexibility

The great advantage that the sport of triathlon has over individual sports is that there is not a focus on one single area of the body, the specific endurance, or the muscles used. Swimming is a tremendous way of achieving overall fitness as it increases strength, endurance and flexibility. However, it focuses primarily on the upper body. Similarly, cycling and running concentrate on the legs and lower body (although many would argue that unless participants also work *specifically* on leg strength, there is little leg strength, as opposed to endurance, to be gained

by endurance running alone). However, a combination of triathlon's three disciplines creates a healthy demand of work spread throughout the body. Swimming, cycling and running all need a good cardiovascular system: a strong heart created by the aerobic and endurance demands of the sports.

Swimming and cycling are also strength-building exercises. Swimming develops strength in the chest, arms, shoulders and back, and cycling the legs and gluteal muscles. Every time you take a stroke in swimming, you are pressing and pulling against resistance; every time you turn a pedal in cycling, you are doing the same. Running up hills also builds strong leg and gluteus muscles.

Body Weight and Body Fat

Once you start training as a triathlete, it is highly likely that you will start to lose weight, and for many people, this is one of most appealing reasons to start training for triathlon. Triathlon is an endurance sport, and training means regular cardiovascular sessions (exercising the heart and lungs). The more hours spent training, the more calories are burned, and the more weight lost. It is actually body fat that will be lost. Body weight is a huge issue with many people, but it is actually the amount of body fat carried that is important. Losing weight is a simple matter of burning off (exercising) more than is taken in (eating). To lose weight, the aim is a negative balance, to put out more than you take in. However, it is necessary to be sensible, and training in an endurance sport does not mean that any amount of any food can be eaten! Certainly, more physical exercise means that more food can be eaten, but if weight loss is one of the aims, then sensible eating and balancing the correct

amounts of protein, carbohydrates and fats is necessary. It is important to dispel the myth that all fat is bad for you. This is just not true, as some fat is essential for health and protecting the body. Very generally, it is the saturated fats that should be avoided (see Chapter 16, Diet and Nutrition).

For many people in the Western world, the quest for eternal youth has become almost a religion. Exercising will not achieve that goal, but it will make you look and feel better. The benefits of training on all three disciplines ensure that bodily appearance will be good. With a concentration on just one sport, appearance can often seem unbalanced; with the training on upper and lower body in triathlon, this imbalance is overcome.

Age is no barrier to healthy living.
© Nigel Farrow

Triathlon's healthy lifestyle means that you can compete for many years! © Nigel Farrow

Older people often complain of feeling that they have little or no energy for every day tasks; a regular training programme in triathlon (although perhaps difficult to begin with as you break the habit of lethargy or laziness) will make you fitter and healthier and will eventually give you more energy during the day. It is important that you do *not* begin by training too hard! Encountering too much fatigue too soon is a recipe for stopping training.

Injury and Boredom

One of the reasons that people report for giving up on a sport is that training has become boring. This is unlikely in triathlon with the necessity of training in all three disciplines. In the unlikely event of injury, then increased emphasis can be put into the disciplines other than where injury is stopping training. However, using the different areas of your body during training is likely to prevent the onset of injuries. Repeating the same movements and exercises all the time can lead to overuse injuries. Runners often encounter problems with knees, shinsplints in the lower leg and tendonitis. Swimmers can be plagued with shoulder problems. Cyclists will often suffer from a lack of mobility. It is far better to be a triathlete and spread the strain.

The normal health benefits of regular exercise can be applied to and multiplied in triathlon training: lowering blood pressure, a lesser chance of developing Type 2 diabetes, lessening the risk of osteoporosis, heart disease and cancer.

Finally, being fit and healthy makes you feel good about yourself. This 'feel good' factor is often understated but is certainly true. People who exercise regularly tend to have a positive outlook on life, and have better resistance to disease. They feel better about themselves and realize that it is because of the inseparability of the mental and physical that they do so.

PART 2
THE TECHNIQUE OF THE THREE DISCIPLINES

CHAPTER 6

THE BASICS OF TECHNIQUE

Skill and Technique

In any sport it is important that technique is excellent. Skill is often defined as 'maintaining technique under pressure'. With the three disciplines in triathlon, it is even more important that technique is excellent. Triathlon is a continuous sport, the three disciplines following immediately after each other, and any accumulated fatigue from one discipline is carried into the next. If technique is excellent, then the fatigue factor is likely to be less of a problem. Overcoming fatigue, cycling and running faster and more efficiently are major factors in a successful race. Technique is not something that should be trained for and practised only at certain times. Good technique should be emphasized by the athlete and the coach in and throughout every training session. The drills ands skills that contribute to good technique are examined in the four chapters on swimming, cycling, running and transition (changing from one discipline to the next).

Economy of Effort

There are no short cuts to having excellent technique. Triathletes come from very different backgrounds and while it will be an initial advantage to bring good technique from one discipline, that good technique must be learned in the other disciplines as well. To be a successful triathlete, it is no longer appropriate to have excellent technique in two disciplines and average technique in the third. Excellence must be carried through all the disciplines. The phrase 'economy of effort' is frequently used when explaining good technique. The less effort that is used to maintain practised and rehearsed technique, the more energy is available for speed.

All the three disciplines are repetitious and demanding sports, and the skills must be efficient. If two triathletes with comparable fitness levels compete against each other, the triathlete with better technique and skills will win. (However, this does not take into account mental toughness and tenacity; see Chapter 17, Mental Attitude.)

Overcoming Resistance

Theories about training for swimming, cycling and running and the technique of each sport have all changed as sports science research discovers more; but there are certain rationales that remain constant.

Successful swimming, cycling and running will be in some part about overcoming resistance:

- resistance of the water in swimming;
- wind, rolling resistance, gravity and aerodynamic forces in cycling;
- wind and impact forces in running.

Technique in all three disciplines must be efficient to produce the least resistance possible. It is a given that extra speed produces extra resistance to overcome and as speed increases good technique is even more important. Any actions that create extra resistance must be avoided:

- swimmers must be in a flat, horizontal position;
- a low position for cyclists will be aerodynamic;
- lateral and vertical deviations should be avoided in running.

Length versus Cadence

The three triathlon disciplines require very different skills, but there are also many similarities. Very generally:

Great Britain international Vanessa Raw demonstrates excellent swim technique.
© Nigel Farrow

Position and technique on the bike add up to economy of effort. © Nigel Farrow

Swimming speed = Stroke length × speed of stroke (cadence)
Cycling speed = Gearing × pedal revolution (cadence)
Running speed = Stride length × stride rate (cadence)

The similarities are immediately apparent. Finding the correct length and cadence is crucial and there is no 'correct' one which suits everybody. Individuals will be best suited according to their particular physical make-up. Caution should be exercised with overgearing (too big) in cycling, stride length (too long) in running, and shortening the stroke to maintain a high turnover in swimming. Again very generally, speed of stride in running, length of stroke in swimming and a combination of gearing and cadence in cycling are the critical factors.

Propulsion and Recovery

With all the disciplines there are phases of propulsion and recovery. Good technique will focus on maximizing propulsion and overcoming the slowing effects of recovery. This is examined in the chapter on each individual sport.

Mobility

Good mobility (flexibility) will be helpful in attaining good technique.

Particularly, length of swimming stroke and an increase in length of the running stride may be enhanced by good mobility, provided that the rate of stroke and of striding does not slow.

Tim Don maintains running form under pressure. © Nigel Farrow

CHAPTER 7

SWIMMING

For newcomers, swimming is the most technical of the three disciplines in triathlon. New triathletes coming from a running or cycling background have to adjust to the necessity of working on technique in swimming before adding the hard work. Long hours in the pool will not make you swim faster unless good swimming technique is evident. All athletes make great physical efforts to improve, but particularly with swimming, an efficient technique must come first. Breaking the stroke down and practising drills and skills are an essential part of becoming an efficient swimmer. Some swimming coaches would add that, unless technique is worked on, a poor stroke with hard effort will actually slow down swimming performance. It is essential that triathlon swimmers allocate sufficient time in the training schedule for technique.

Stroke counting is a useful exercise for improving front crawl. The swimmer should count the number of strokes needed to cover 50m while checking the time taken. For example, if a swimmer swims 10 × 50m counting strokes and averages 37 seconds he should then try to reduce the number of strokes while maintaining or improving the 37 seconds time. Stroke counting is an important indicator of tiredness.

There is a further complication of competing in open water outdoors, and some observers will say that swimming in a wetsuit bears little resemblance to swimming in a pool. This is untrue. There are differences in pool and open water swimming, but in general good pool swimmers make good open water and triathlon swimmers. However, there are some additions and adjustments that can be made in training to deal with these conditions.

Front Crawl

Front crawl is the fastest and most efficient of the swimming strokes. All swimming

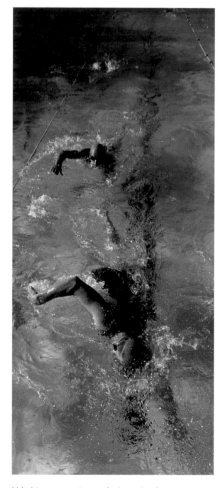

Working on swim technique is always necessary. © *Nigel Farrow*

Swimming in wetsuits adds a new dimension. © *Nigel Farrow*

strokes are permitted in triathlon, but most competitors choose front crawl. The force is directed backwards and there is continuous propulsion. The flat body position and good streamlining make front crawl particularly efficient for long distance swimming.

Body Position

The body should be in a flat, horizontal position, stretched and streamlined just below the surface with the hips slightly lower than the shoulders. The pull should be within the body width and the kick within the body depth; it is essential that the kick is used for balance. Wearing a wetsuit gives extra buoyancy and anything more than a light 'feather' kick to balance the stroke will mean wasted energy. The face should be in the water, hips close to the surface, back straight and legs under the surface.

The head position is the key to the body position along with the balancing leg kick. The head should be in line with the body in a natural position with the eyes looking down (at about 45 degrees) and with the water level breaking between hairline and the middle of the head. The head is steady and central except when breathing and all swimmers should avoid attempting to swim higher in the water by lifting the head or arching the back.

Faster swimming is achieved by a combination of streamlining and applying propulsive forces effectively.

Poor streamlining is caused by several factors.

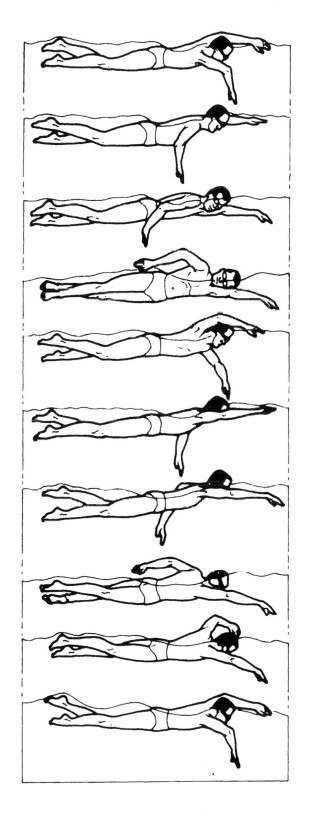

Front crawl, side view.

- Sideways movement: lifting the head too far to the side when breathing, pulling outside the body line and/or a wide arm recovery.
- Vertical movement: lifting and lowering the head to breathe, pushing down too much as the hand enters the water, and pushing up too much at the end of the stroke.
- Over-rotation: poor mobility in the shoulders, so needing to roll to recover the arms. Proper, efficient rotation is a necessity.

Rotation (Body Roll)

Rotation will make front crawl streamlined and efficient. The shoulders and upper body roll from side to side as one arm begins its pull and the other recovers. This rotation makes it easier to swim front crawl efficiently. As the right arm enters the water the swimmer rolls onto the right shoulder. When the right arm extends the swimmer should 'ride' on that arm to give the hand and forearm a good 'feel' for the water. At the same time the swimmer lifts the left shoulder higher out of the water as the left arm finishes its stroke and begins to recover. The left shoulder continues to go higher as the left arm reaches its highest point in the recovery. At the same time the right arm is coming under the body and the right shoulder is at its deepest point. At this point of maximum rotation the line between the two shoulders will be almost directly perpendicular to the surface of the pool, straight up and down. As the stroke continues the shoulders will reverse positions. The right shoulder will come up as the right arm finishes the underwater stroke and the left shoulder will come down as the left arm enters the water and starts to pull.

The Advantages of Rotation

- It uses the big shoulder, chest and back muscles rather than just the smaller arm muscles.

Front crawl, front view.

- It allows the pulling arm and hand to go deeper and get a better 'grip' on the water.
- Stroke length is longer, 'catching' further in front and stretching further back.
- Recovery is easier as the recovering shoulder is higher (particularly for those with little flexibility in the shoulders).
- It cuts in half the resistance of the upper body in the water.

Drills to Assist and Accentuate Body Roll

- Catch-up, where one arm is extended in front as the other pulls through, is good for working on body roll to the non-breathing side, as is single-arm pulling, but be sure to completely roll in both directions.
- Kicking on the side with the lower arm extended and the other by the side simulates the body movement. Progressions are to change from side to side, using a front crawl stroke, every 12, 10, 8, 6 and 4 kicks.

This is a particularly demanding drill for triathletes who do not have swimming as their background discipline, but is well worth persevering with as the improvement gained and the confidence of being able to deal with what feels like an uncomfortable position and environment pays dividends when athletes are faced with a demanding open water swim.

- The 3 + 6 drill. This is similar to the drill described above.

Three arm strokes are taken and then the swimmer continues to stay on the side with one arm extended in front. The swimmer then takes six kicks while the arm is extended and the body is on the side. This is then repeated. By doing this, the swimmer exaggerates the rotation and with every three arm strokes a 180-degree body rotation has taken place.

Leg Action

Despite having to wear wetsuits for many open water swims, it is important for athletes to work on the leg kick during training because neglecting the legs will lead to decreased efficiency. In hotter conditions, triathletes will have to swim open water events without a wetsuit.

The main function of the legs is to achieve and stabilize a horizontal body position, and to balance the arm action. The legs move close together in an alternating vertical movement utilizing the whole of the leg with the knees alternately bending and straightening, with the feet extended and the toes pointed. The ankles need to be loose and flexible throughout.

The kick starts at the hip and the thigh is swept down. The knee and ankle joints are relaxed, allowing the pressure of the water beneath the leg to flex the knee and push the toes upwards and inwards. As the downbeat nears completion the legs are snapped straight and the feet outwards. The whip-like action brings the largest area of the feet in contact with the water pressure in a backwards and downwards direction.

The leg then rebounds upwards after the downbeat is completed. It will be relaxed at the knee and ankle so that the water pressure above the leg maintains it in an extended position as it travels upwards. The soles of the feet and backs of the legs press upwards and backwards against the water. Only the heels break the surface and the feet should not come out of the water. The kick will be less than 12 inches (30cm) deep, not so deep as to create resistance but deep enough to balance the body, and it should be maintained within body depth. Turning the toes inwards is a natural reaction. Flexibility of the ankles is important as inflexible ankles will create resistance and drag. The more flexible are the ankles, the more effective will be the kick.

As the swim discipline is longer than a swimming pool sprint, most triathletes use a two-beat kick, or variation of it, as it is economical and energy saving. In essence, the leg action complements the arm action, and is almost solely a balancing one, often looking like a drift of the legs. However, it is a technique that is particularly advantageous to middle- and long-distance swimmers and triathletes.

It is important to condition the legs during training. Neglecting the leg kick leads to it becoming less efficient in performing the important function of stabilizing and balancing. It is important to develop an efficient leg kick right form the start.

The leg kick is important for stabilizing and balance. © Nigel Farrow

FRONT CRAWL CHECKLIST

The whole stroke

- Body streamlined in near-horizontal position throughout the stroke
- Avoid lifting of head and shoulders
- Avoid radical body movements: up and down or a snaking motion
- Feet deep enough for effective kicking action
- Proper stroke mechanics with both arms
- Balanced, maximum power with both arms
- Roll of body, including shoulders and hips, about the long axis
- Avoid wasted efforts that do not aid in propulsion or breathing
- One arm always applying effective force to water; avoid 'stop and go'

Arms

- Arms enter water at shoulder-width: hand first, little finger up and elbow slightly bent
- Momentum from the recovery causes the elbow to lift and the arm to sink towards an early catch as the wrist rotates so that the palm is flat down
- Wrist action permits early catch
- Elbow up early in pull; remain up for as long as possible and avoid dropping the elbow
- Swimmer should have the sensation of pushing the elbow up and forward
- Palm and inside of forearm in vertical plane that is roughly parallel to pool and wall early in the pull and for as long as possible
- Water held behind hand and arm for as long as possible with minimum of slippage
- Wrist action permits palm of the hand to be held flat against the water for as long as possible during the upsweep
- Swimmer should have the feeling of moving water towards the feet throughout the stroke with a feeling of pressure on the hand and forearm
- Acceleration of 'pull-push' from relatively slow catch to fast finish
- Elbow leads recovery with the hand following
- High elbow recovery with elbow always higher than the hand
- Arm relaxes for as much as possible during most of the recovery

Legs

- Toes generally pointed throughout the kick
- Flexibility of the knee permits the thigh to start a downkick while the foot continues upwards and the knee bends
- Accelerating downwards thrust of the foot should result in complete knee extension
- Noticeable whip action; ankle hyper-extended during downbeat
- Ankle flexibility noticeable
- Flexibility of the knee permits the thigh to start the upbeat while the foot continues downwards and the knee straightens
- Maximum vertical spread of the feet should be 12 inches (30cm) depending on the age and size of the swimmer
- Kick helps maintain body alignment

Breathing

- Head turned to side by rotating neck on longitudinal body axis
- Breathing coincides with body roll
- Inhale while mouth is below calm water level, in trough of wave created by the head
- Body roll and head turn towards non-breathing side should be sufficient to balance the stroke

Kicking Drills

1   Using a float, sometimes with the head held high for resistance-conditioning
2   Arms extended, hands overlapped, face down between arms, breathe to the front on the 6th kick
3   Arms at side, face in water, breathe to alternate sides every 6th kick
4   Pearl-diver-breaststroke arms, front crawl kick
5   Extended doggy-paddle
6   Kicking on the side: one arm spearing out in front, other arm lying along the side. Change to other side using a full stroke every 12, 10, 8, 6, or 4 kicks (see Drills to Assist and Accentuate Body Roll).
7   Kicking with fins, which helps to develop flexibility
8   Vertical kick in deep water with hands both up and down.

Techniques to Emphasize in the Kick

- Kick continuously
- Kick with legs long and flexible knees and ankles
- Kick within the body depth
- Kick from the hips

Arm Action

The main propulsive force is derived from the arms and the action is an alternating one with continuous movement, resembling climbing a rope with one arm pulling while the other recovers.

Entry

Arm entry is in front of the head, between the outside line of the body (the shoulder) and the midline, ensuring that the hand does not cross over the mid-point. The arm is not completely straight, being slightly flexed downwards from elbow to fingertips. The thumb and fingertips enter the water first, with the hand 'slicing' into the water. The hand then goes down this entry hole and quickly follows with the forearm.

One arm enters the water as the other is just over halfway through the pull phase.

Catch

This is where the grip on the water takes place and an efficient catch is important. The hand reaches forwards in a straight line just a few inches under the surface while the other arm completes its underwater phase. *Care should be taken to prevent the elbow dropping below the hand as it reaches forward.* The 'dropped elbow' is one of the single biggest reasons for an inefficient stroke.

It is here that the rotation of the upper arm starts to achieve a high elbow position, since this elbow bend is a vital leverage factor which increases power. This rotation of the arm along with body rotation ensures that the shoulder and chest muscles are used.

Arms and Propulsion

The hand puts pressure on the water, the palm of the hand pressing slightly out and downwards. The hand then pitches slightly inwards towards the centre of the body with the edge of the thumb leading. The elbow is pointing towards the side of the pool. At the midline of the body the fingers point towards the bottom of the pool and push backwards. The thumb passes very close to the legs in a pushing-away movement.

The Myth of the S-shaped Pull

Much has been written of the arm action as an S-shaped pull. However, it is much more a direct backwards pull or pushing-away with the hand appearing to be 'fixed' on the water. The myth perhaps arose with very young swimmers not having the necessary strength to hold the correct pull and push line. In some swimmers, there may be a very flat 'S' shape.

Release

As the hand passes the thigh the pressure is released and the momentum of the upsweep carries the hand upwards and outwards from the water with minimal resistance. Exit is with the little finger first.

Recovery

The elbow leads into the recovery phase and should remain slightly flexed leading the wrist and hand out of the water. The hand should exit 'where it went in' giving the feeling of pulling the body over the entry 'hole'. The forearm moves close to the head and the hand stays below the elbow going towards the entry phase.

High Elbow Recovery

A feature of a good front crawl should be the high elbow position, not only during the pull phase, but also through recovery. This encourages good balance in the recovery and good rotation along the axis of the body, helping streamlining. Tightness in the shoulder will obviously affect the stroke. There are three main types of recovery:

1 high elbow, wrist pick-up, placing forward of the hand;
2 high elbow, swinging round of the lower arm;
3 straight swinging action of the whole arm.

Every aspect of technique is important in being able to swim like Michael Phelps.
© Nigel Farrow

Wearing a wetsuit with full arms may lead to slightly restricted mobility on the recovery phase. More flexible materials are now being used in their manufacture, making them less restricting than in the past.

Techniques to Emphasize for Arms and Co-ordination

- Elbows up on the recovery and stroke
- Start the recovery in the shoulder and elbow
- Hand under and just outside the elbow on recovery
- Hand, wrist and elbow enter the water in that order
- Arm falls downwards as it passes the shoulder in recovery
- Turn the chin to follow the shoulder roll to breathe
- Inhale through the mouth, exhale through the mouth or mouth and nose
- Look at the water surface just in front of the mouth when breathing
- Begin to turn the head to breathe when the stroking arm on the non-breathing side enters the water

Drills for Arms and Co-ordination

1. Stretch body swims, streamlined, no breathing
2. One-arm swims with one arm extended, no breathing
3. Rolling doggy-paddle
4. Single arm with free arm at side. Breathe to non-stroking side
5. Catch-up with a definite pause
6. Full stroke with thumbs touching armpit on recovery
7. Kicking on side changing to other side with full stroke
8. Swim, touching thumb to thighs before release
9. Swim, brushing ears with shoulders
10. Keeping head still, swim exaggerating roll of body
11. One arm extended out of the water while opposite arm strokes continuously
12. Using fists, emphasizing pulling with arms
13. Fists on downsweep and insweep, hands open on upsweep

Fist swimming is used to:

- develop the power phase being executed in a straight line
- correct any glide-away of hands after entry
- ensure the stroke is not performed too far from the body
- stop the hand trailing the elbow
- prevent an arm recovery that may be too wide and flat.

Breathing

Breathing has to be taught in swimming because it must come at a time when it interferes least with the stroke. Breathing contributes nothing to propulsion, and swimmers can only go so far without breathing. There is a smooth, controlled turn of the head to the side, with the side of the face kept in the water. The head turns as body rotation takes place with the face and entire body, including shoulders and hips, rolling towards the breathing side without moving the head away from the midline. The amount of roll should be about 45 degrees on the breathing side and slightly less on the other. The head begins to turn for a breath when the hand opposite the breathing side enters the water. This is the natural place to breathe as the roll of the body allows the face to be exposed to the air with the least amount of head movement. The head should be turned and not lifted and it is important that the head returns to the body line before the entering arm has passed the face.

Bi-lateral breathing uses both sides, usually alternately every third arm pull. This style of breathing is useful for correcting faults and causes less interference to the stroke in general. It can be used to correct a swimmer who pulls harder with one arm, has a weak leg kick or is having difficulty balancing the stroke. It is essential for competitive swimmers to be able to see both sides without breaking stroke. Alternate breathing involves breathing every stroke cycle and breath-holding can be a good conditioner as well as working on the start and finish of a race.

Some Faults and Corrections

Mechanically, front crawl is the most efficient and thus the fastest known stroke. It is also very natural and normally the first stroke that is taught. However, there are a number of common mistakes made (see table opposite).

FAULTS AND CORRECTIONS

Faults and problems	Corrections
Flat	Turn the thumb inwards; doing this will raise the elbow
Close to body	Swim close to the wall; you will have to lift the elbow to avoid touching the wall
Flip at finish	Imagine that you are taking your hand out of your pocket, with the palm of the hand in contact with the leg
Entry	
Flat, splash	Hold your head up and watch the hand entry
Wide	Imagine that your hands are entering the water having crossed over in front of your head
Dropped elbow	Turn your thumb downwards as you enter and don't over-reach
Gliding on arm	Speed up your stroke slightly. Quick pull – and breathe late
Catch	
Dropped elbow	Imagine that you are pulling over a barrel in the water. Keep your elbow high and push away hard
Deep catch	Maintain your hand position near the surface. Keep high in front rather than dropping down deep
Armstroke	
Cross over	Enter your hands into the water outside the body
Straight arm	Bend your elbow to 90 degrees
Hand near chest	Fix the elbow above the hand and wrist and pull deeper with a bigger angle
Pull wide	Cross over the mid-line of the head and body slightly
Short finish	Attempt to keep your hand in the water for longer. Aim for your thumb to reach down to the thigh – push hard with your hand and flip the fingers and hand backwards at the very end of the push
Long finish	Shorten the second half of the push, keep the elbow up and try to let your thumb maintain contact with body or costume
Body Position	
Head high	Look at the line on the bottom of the pool
Head low	Try to keep your eyebrows at the water level
Shoulders flat	Breathe every three arm strokes rather than every two (bilateral breathing)
Shoulder-up – windmill	Extend the arm reach in front on entry, and rotate the whole body rather than just the shoulders
Stop arm/leg crossover	Change the side to which you breathe. Also work on a shallow and fast kick
Kick	
Too big	Try to lock your knees when kicking, and keep the sole of the foot in the water
Too small	Use fins in training and kick strongly. Kick on the side as well as on the front; allow the sole of the foot to come out of the water
Breathing	
Forward look	Breathe later in the stroke, perhaps just before the recovery starts, and breathe to the side
Back look	Breathe early and look slightly forward
Poor timing	Breathe on the opposite side from that to which you are accustomed, or when the opposite arm is extended

CHAPTER 8

CYCLING

Many experts believe that the cycling discipline is the equalizer or trade-off in triathlon. Certainly, it is usually the longest part of the race and is the only discipline where significant advantages in performance can be gained by close attention to the bike and bike equipment, and also paying attention to the importance of a 'good' riding position.

Triathlon has certainly contributed to the sport of cycling itself. Aerobars or tri-bars were first used in triathlon before being allowed in cycling time trials. Only in 1991 were tri-bars allowed in cycling competition and almost immediately long-standing records fell by significant margins. This is particularly important in triathlon because, unless the competition is for elite competitors where drafting (following closely behind another competitor to take advantage of less wind resistance) is allowed, the cycle portion is effectively a time trial: athlete against the clock.

The aerodynamics of the bike and the rider's position are vital. Clearly, the less energy that is required to overcome wind resistance, gravity and rolling resistance, the more energy will be available for riding as fast as possible and as economically as possible. That way there will be energy remaining for the next element, the start of the run. Overcoming wind resistance, particularly, is far more important in cycling than running as the speed on the bike is significantly faster.

The Bike

The bike and the triathlete must fit each other perfectly. The riding and racing position has to combine comfort, mechanical

Toby Radcliffe shows excellent riding position and aerodynamic form.

efficiency and good aerodynamics. It must also allow the athlete to be able to alter style, position and technique to train and compete on courses with different conditions in surface, gradient, severity and distance. Setting up riding and position instructions can only be guidelines as everybody will have individual preferences as well as body shapes and types. However, for the novice triathlete, there have to be starting points to work from. Any adjustment or re-adjustment in riding position must be made gradually as any radical changes will lead to soreness and possibly injury. This is particularly important for saddle height where adjustments should never be more than half a centimetre at a time.

As discussed in Chapter 2, the actual size of the bicycle is not all-important. The adjustments that can be made to the equipment provide a lot of leeway although advice from a reputable bike mechanic or cycle shop should always be sought. The four major adjustments that can be made are:

1 saddle height;
2 saddle front and rear position;
3 handlebar height;
4 handlebar forward and back position, including stem length.

The Riding Position

1 Set the height of the saddle.
2 Ensure the saddle is level.
3 Set the forward and backwards position of the saddle.
4 Estimate length of the handlebar stem.
5 Set the 'tilt' of the handlebars.
6 Fix position of brake-levers on handlebars.
7 Set height of the handlebars.

When the riding position is set, it should be checked again in case any single adjustment has affected others. Again, the height of the saddle is vital. The three points of contact from rider to bike are: bike saddle and rider's backside, bike pedals and rider's feet, bike handlebars and rider's hands. Using tri-bars adds the forearms as a fourth point of contact (they rest on the tri-bar).

To cycle faster, it is necessary to minimize and overcome the resistances that slow us down. These are air resistance and friction (plus gravity on hills).

Air resistance is the main factor limiting speed, as frictional forces are largely determined by design and manufacture. Some of the friction resistance can be overcome by very high air pressure and use of narrow tyres; the less contact with the ground, the less resistance. Riding efficiency is maintained by pedalling action and riding position. As novice triathletes gain more experience, cycling technique

---

CYCLING POSITION PROBLEMS AND SOLUTIONS

Problem	Possible causes
Pain in crotch, groin	Saddle too high, saddle tilted, too many rpm, irregular or infrequent training, saddle too wide, too narrow, too hard
Pain in shoulders, arms, neck	Wrong stem length, stem too low, weak lower back, not tilting head to one side, saddle tilted down, unaccustomed to crash-hat
Pain in hands	Too much weight on arms, staying too long in one position
Knee pain (not from accident)	Pedal cadence too fast, wrong saddle height, using too big gears too soon, cleat angle wrong, pronation or structural problems, old injuries, cold air on uncovered legs
Hitting inside of ankle on crank arm	Excessive pronation, cleat rotation
'Bouncing' in the saddle at high rpm	Incorrect saddle height, tense upper body, poor pedal stroke
Feeling bunched up	Too-short top tube or stem
Shifting position on saddle	Saddle too high or tilted incorrectly
Tight calf muscles	Fore-aft cleat position incorrect, rigid ankles, overly pointed toes

Emma Dearsley rides on tri-bars, Toby Radcliffe on top of bars.

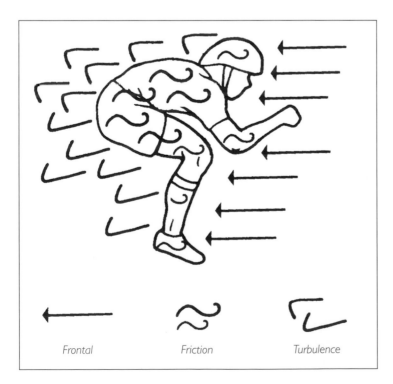

Frontal   Friction   Turbulence

will change, and what feels most comfortable is not always necessarily best. The table on page 37 indicates common faults and possible answers (*see* Steve Trew *Triathlon, A Training Manual,* Crowood Press 2001).

Air Resistance and Drag

Air resistance and drag can be loosely divided into three areas.

Frontal Resistance How much area of the rider's body is in the wind? The smaller the area is, the less the wind resistance will be. By changing shape, the cyclist influences this resistance.

Surface Friction How smooth is the overall surface of the rider and the bike over which the air flows? Loose clothing will affect this greatly.

Turbulence This is very similar to surface friction as it is largely created by the surface. It is the amount of disruption of

Air resistance can be frontal, frictional, or due to turbulence.

the air behind the body and the bike and is influenced by the shape, aerodynamics and smoothness of the bike and rider. In many ways, the shape should be similar to that of the downhill skier.

Shoe and Foot Position

The ball of the foot should be directly above the pedal axle and the cleat or click-in should be adjusted accordingly. If the position is set too far forward it will lead to calf and toe cramping; if set too far back it will create an uneconomical, up-and-down pedal action.

Gears and Cadence (Pedalling Speed)

The correct choice and use of gears and cadence is essential for fast cycling. It is important therefore to make the right decisions about the size of the gear and the speed of pedal revolutions.
The two wrong choices are:

1 selecting too big a gear and being forced to pedal so slowly against the high resistance that fatigue is almost immediate (particularly in triathlon as the run discipline follows the bike discipline);
2 selecting so small a gear, creating 'over-spinning', that however high your cadence you are going to make little progress.

It is unusual that these extremes of gear selection are chosen although the choice of slightly too high or low gears is frequent. There is no single correct gearing and cadence that suits everyone although there are a number of points that should be considered.

• Low (easy) gears will tend to develop good suppleness and flexibility in the legs and particularly the ankles.
• Recovery tends to be at a faster rate on low (easy) gears than high gears.
• High (big) gears rely on strength.

USE OF GEARS

110 inches or more	Downhill Very fast flat roads, wind behind
90–108 inches	Steady fast pedalling on open, flat roads in good conditions Wind behind. Triathlon, time trial
86–94 inches	Road racing, some training Triathlon/time trial on undulating roads Track work
70–85 inches	Road racing (sitting in bunch, coasting) and most hard training
60–65 inches	Winter, commuting, training Easy riding, touring While racing, most uphills
50–60 inches	For steep uphills (1-in-10 or steeper)
50 inches or less	Very steep slopes

HOW SPEED (MPH) IS DETERMINED BY CADENCE (RPM) AND GEARING

Gear	Pedal revolutions per minute			
	80	90	100	110
42 × 17	15.9mph	17.9mph	19.9mph	21.9mph
42 × 16	16.9mph	19mph	21.1mph	23.2mph
42 × 15	18.1mph	20.4mph	22.6mph	24.9mph
42 × 14	19.3mph	21.7mph	24.1mph	26.5mph
52 × 17	19.8mph	22.2mph	24.7mph	27.2mph
52 × 16	20.9mph	23.6mph	26.2mph	28.8mph
52 × 15	22.4mph	25.2mph	28mph	30.8mph
52 × 14	23.8mph	26.8mph	29.8mph	32.8mph
53 × 16	21.1mph	23.8mph	26.5mph	29.1mph
53 × 15	22.6mph	25.4mph	28.3mph	31.1mph
53 × 14	24.3mph	27.3mph	30.3mph	33.4mph
53 × 13	26.2mph	29.5mph	32.7mph	36mph

The four phases of the pedalling technique.

A closer look at pedalling technique.

- It is less stressful to knee joints to choose low gears and fast cadence rather than high gears and low cadence.
- Fast rides have been done using high and low gears, however, triathletes

have to run after the bike section and overuse of big gears may be detrimental to this.

It is suggested that a cadence of between 90 and 100 revolutions per minute coupled

with the appropriate gearing to match this is the ideal. This may well be the mid-point or trade-off. However, it is not necessarily appropriate for everybody. Note should be taken of strength and speed, cadence, heart rate, perceived effort (how hard do you think you are working?), fatigue and individual knowledge of how different cadences and gearing affect the ability to run after you have finished cycling.

Self-analysis

- If the heartbeat is high, the cadence is too high and the gearing too low.
- If the leg muscles are aching and fatigued, the gearing is too high and the cadence too low. The chart on page 39 may help to indicate the range of gears to choose in particular racing and training circumstances.

What Does Different Gearing Mean?

Very generally, gearing is defined as the distance covered by one full revolution of the pedals. To work out how far that distance is, the following formula is used.

Multiply the number of teeth on the chainwheel by the diameter of the wheel, then divide by the number of teeth on the rear sprocket. This will give the distance travelled in inches. For example, 54 teeth on the chainwheel, a 27-inch diameter wheel and 18 teeth on the rear sprocket gives

$$\frac{54}{18} \times 27 = 81 \text{ inches travelled with each pedal revolution,}$$

it is then fairly simple to work out how far is travelled in a minute or an hour by knowing the cadence (revolutions per minute or rpm). A much smaller gear with 42 teeth on the chainwheel, a 27-inch diameter wheel and 28 teeth on the rear sprocket gives

$$\frac{42}{28} \times 27 = 41 \text{ inches travelled with each pedal revolution.}$$

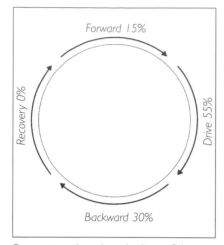

Force output through each phase of the pedal cycle.

Experiment with different gearing and different rpms to discover the best option for each individual. Riders' fitness levels will determine this.

Pedalling Technique

It is more efficient and less fatiguing to pedal in a circular action rather than an up-and-down action. More muscle groups and fibres are recruited by the circular motion and muscle fatigue will be delayed if this technique is used: the triathlete will therefore be less fatigued at the start of the run discipline.

However, a circling motion does not imply that as much effort will be used in pulling the pedals up as in pushing them down. Bigger, stronger muscle groups are used in the downward thrust and as the pedals are necessarily opposite to each other, less effort will be required to bring the pedals upwards as long as a strong pressure is exerted downwards. It is essential that pressure is maintained at the possible 'dead spots' at the very top and bottom of the pedal action (see diagram). Points to help here are to think of scraping something off the shoe at the bottom of the action, and pushing the knee and

Excellent cornering technique shown by Alistair Brownlee. © Nigel Farrow

foot forward at the top of the pedal action. A smooth transition between each phase will ensure that the pedal action is correct.

Use of Brakes

Normally both brakes should be applied together and with the same pressure. However, applying the brakes while cornering may make the rear wheel slip away, as the action of cornering itself reduces tyre grip on the road surface. Slowing and braking will exaggerate this.

Cornering

Riding in anything but a straight line will feel dangerous initially, but there are techniques which help make corner-taking easier. Less speed will be lost as you gain experience and confidence.

- Adjust your speed and hold the brake levers before the corner or bend. Too much pressure on the brakes during cornering while the bike is leaning may cause the bike to slip.

Out of the saddle to climb.

OUT-OF-SADDLE RIDING

1 Approaching the hill, rider changes down a gear and continues to pedal.
2 As bottom of hill is reached, rider is out of the saddle and presses down hard on the pedals in order to start fast up the hill.
3 Staying out of the saddle, rider pushes down and pulls up on pedals, developing a steady rhythm and controlling breathing.
4 If the hill is long, rider changes down (if needed) and sits well back in the saddle, pulling on handlebars for extra leverage, pushing and pulling on pedals.
5 Rider maintains speed over the crest of the hill, usually staying out of the saddle.
6 Rider does not slow down on start of descent, but stays in the saddle, changes up a gear, controls breathing.
7 Rider stays seated in a good aerodynamic position on descent, continues to pedal at normal cadence and changes up gears where appropriate.

• It is best to follow a straight a line in and out of the corner. Select the line to follow before you start cornering.
• Be aware of road conditions after the corner to ensure you select the correct gear for minimum loss of speed.
• Keep the inside pedal down and the outside pedal up if it is necessary to stop pedalling through the bend or corner.
• Press down on the outside pedal; this will give a good tyre grip on the road.
• Lean your body and bike into the bend or corner. This will help to stop the bike drifting outwards and out of control.
• Stay relaxed but in control.
• Be aware of dangerous road conditions: wet, ice, grease, gravel or sand or loose stones on the road. Metal road surfaces are particularly dangerous, as are roads where rain has fallen on greasy surfaces after a long period of dry weather.

Climbing Hills and Slopes

Steep hills will probably make the rider lift out of the saddle, but appropriate selection of gears should be used to climb easier hills. Gear selection will become easier with experience. Many climbs will be 'in-between'; in this case switch between seated climbing and out-of-the-saddle riding.

Note the seated position on easy climbs.

CHAPTER 9

RUNNING

The Running Action

Good technique is crucial in running during a triathlon, as the athlete is coming into the final discipline already fatigued from swimming and cycling. The technique of any endurance running is modified sprinting, but the action of running has to be efficient to lessen any unnecessary use of energy.

There is a propulsive phase and a recovery phase in running.

The propulsive phase starts as soon as the foot makes contact with the ground during a running stride. The whole of the bodyweight is impacted upon the foot as the hips and trunk are moved forward over the foot; and the hip, knee and ankle stretch out.

The recovery phase begins with the foot leaving the ground. The foot is pulled upwards and the thigh swings forward and through until it is almost parallel to the ground. The lower part of the leg then comes forward as the thigh begins to move downwards. The whole leg then sweeps backwards and downwards until the foot strikes the ground again.

The upper body remains upright or leaning slightly forward. Energy can be wasted by getting away from forward, horizontal progress by lifting and dropping the head and hips. By always thinking of keeping the hips up high, triathletes avoid the body sagging down, particularly as they get progressively more tired, and do not have to use valuable energy to lift the body back up again. The arm action should match the leg action; left arm coming forward at the same time as the right leg and vice versa, in an equal and opposite action and reaction. The arm movement should be kept relaxed and rhythmic, moving backwards and forwards in a straight line with the hands loosely cupped and the thumbs resting on the fingers. A powerful, strong arm-drive will dictate how fast the legs move and the length of stride. Just as a good leg kick in swimming is important for balance and maintaining a good position, so is a strong upper body and arm drive in running.

Any sideways arm movement will detract from economy of running. The arms balance and drive the legs so the arms should swing forward and back rather than sideways. The arm action should be economical and relaxed, but the speed and height of the arm swing (particularly on the back swing) contribute to running speed.

Experienced runners check their action and body position frequently; particularly head position, upright running, cadence and foot strike.

Hip and lower body mobility will also influence the speed and efficiency of running. Poor mobility will inhibit stride length. Good running technique involves the flexion and extension and some rotation of the ankle, knee and hip. As previously stated, in running:

Speed = Stride length × Stride rate.

If we wish to improve either of these factors, then we must increase the range of movement in the joints and the strength in the running muscle groups.

The Effects of Cycling on Running

In the early stages of triathlon running, cycling will have a big impact on the speed of running. In cycling, the legs have been circling continually at around 80 to 100 revolutions per minute (rpm). There has been no impact on the ground. As the run discipline starts, that circular movement becomes an up-and-down one with impact and jarring on each step. The impact of each step can multiply body weight by as much as four times. Even with experienced runners, running after cycling can be challenging and difficult. It is important that cycling cadence is not too slow (often caused by using too big a gear) as muscle memory will come into play. If the cadence on the bike section has been 60 or 70rpm, rather than 80 to 100rpm, then that cadence will be remembered when the run starts and the athlete will run at that leg speed. Indications are that successful fast running requires a leg turn over of at least 160 per minute (both left and right legs). Dividing the 160 strike rate by two, this equates nicely with the 80 to 100rpm cycle cadence. Selecting too big a gear on cycling may have a negative effect on running speed.

Economy of Effort

Good Technique versus Poor Technique

A good runner will have:

- an upright running action, a steady head position looking forward and level
- a high knee lift, a good stride length, a foot strike towards the front of the foot
- a fast stride frequency (180 foot touches plus per minute of running), and maintenance of that stride frequency throughout the run.

Emma Dearsley shows all the necessary requirements of the propulsive and recovery phase for running.

Note the slight lean forwards.

Note the strong arm drive both forwards and backwards.

A strong arm action is even more important on hills.

Good technique in running is important especially after cycling.

In addition a runner with good technique will avoid tense or tight shoulders and neck as this will contribute to early fatigue. Breathing should be controlled; holding the breath or very shallow breathing will also lead to early fatigue. This can be controlled by a focus on breathing *out* rather than a concentration on breathing *in*.

An emphasis on keeping the hips forward and high will ensure that stride length is good. Dropped hips are caused either by cumulative fatigue from the cycle discipline or weak core muscles.

Conversely, a poor runner will have:

- a seated running action, the body bobbing up and down
- an unsteady head position with the eyes looking down rather than forward and level
- the hips dropped, the backside stuck out, a low knee lift, an over-long or very short stride length
- a heel strike with the foot under or behind the knee, a low stride frequency (less than 140 foot touches per minute), a slowing of stride frequency as fatigue becomes apparent.

Heel striking is associated with over-striding. It creates a braking effect as the body's centre of gravity will be behind the foot strike each time. A tremendous amount of energy is then required to bring the body weight back in front, basically a 'lift' each stride. Impact injuries are also frequent with an overlong stride length. Leaning back rather than forward will also contribute to the braking effect.

Running Drills

Running drills isolate individual aspects of the running action. They require co-ordination and balance and are carried out for very short distances to avoid fatigue, when technique may break down. Running drills may not seem to be as important as swimming drills, but remember that running is the final discipline when tiredness has already set in. Practising running drills is important to ensure that run technique is maintained even through that fatigue.

The most important parts of the running action are: high lift of the upper leg, paw down and pull back of the lead leg, full extension and lift of the rear leg, and a full range of arm movement. That is, for the legs and feet progressively: toe up, heel up, knee up, reach out, claw back. By working hard on running drills, the usual range of movement will be extended and the likelihood is that foot-strike will be more powerful. As running is a high impact activity, running on grass is advisable in the

---

TOP TIP

An upright running action can be encouraged by thinking of cotton attached to head and pulling up, by pushing the hips forward, and by leaning forward from the feet.

All the attributes of an excellent runner are seen here.

early stages of running drills. Impact and the chance of soreness and injury will be reduced by training on a softer surface.

A simple activity such as **skipping** is a good warm-up that will also need some co-ordination. Gradually increasing the height of each skip will require more and more leg strength, and this basic activity will supply two of the essential needs for running: co-ordination and leg power.

Improving mobility will ensure that the stride length during the run will be increased without having to resort to heel-striking and the accompanying 'braking' effect.

Lunges will improve mobility and will also have an effect on leg strength. A

lunge is basically a very long step forward while keeping the upper body upright and lowering the hips towards the floor (the back leg knee should not touch the floor). This lunge stretches the muscles in the upper legs and backside and also strengthens these areas when the rear leg is pulled forwards and upwards into the next step or lunge. Each lunge should be held for a count of two.

Speed of stride is the single most important factor in fast running. Practising the **heel flicks** drill emphasizes the necessary speed of stride. The drill is running with very short strides and flicking the heels upwards to try to make contact with the gluteal muscles (backside). It is important to emphasize the speed of the flick-ups while keeping the upper leg (from hip to knee) perpendicular to the floor. There should be further emphasis on having as little 'resting' contact with the ground as possible. As soon as the foot makes contact with the ground, it should be lifted.

A further progression in the heel-flick drill is to combine two running steps followed by one heel flick up. The **1, 2, flick drill** will demand more co-ordination into this drill: two short, fast strides are followed by a flick up as the third stride. This drill requires and emphasizes good co-ordination and it may be necessary to practise it by walking through the drill in the early stages of learning it.

Working on **rapid foot movement** is one the most important aspects of training for fast running. A fast cadence is essential. Take very short steps pushing off from the ground with the toes pointing downwards and barely lifting from the ground. This must be performed as fast as possible for 20 to 30 repetitions before opening up the stride and running out.

The **high knee drill** is used to lift knees and open up the running stride but also to work further on rapid foot and leg movement, reducing the amount of time spent in contact with the ground (as described above). Any extra ground contact time absorbs energy and should be avoided. Concentration is needed to focus on both aspects. The knees are brought up high by bounding upwards with each stride and foot contact. It is important to

maintain good overall running technique with this drill and not lean backwards as the knees come up. Looking forwards and slightly upwards will help with this. The speed of performing the high knee drill can be gradually increased as confidence is gained and the power and drive of the arms should also be increased as the drill progresses.

Ballet Kick or Kick Through

With the body weight taken on one leg, the other leg is kicked upwards to the opposite hand; so with the weight on the left leg, a straight right leg kick up to left hand. The weight-bearing leg is raised onto the toes for a greater range of mobility. This drill is best practised slowly at first, by walking through, to maintain good co-ordination before going through more quickly. It is important to emphasize 'light feet'.

Sideways Running (Crossover Drill)

The co-ordination of running sideways with the legs crossing in front of and behind each other may seem easy, but this drill is effective if co-ordination is a problem. A gradual progression with speed of movement coupled with using the arms as a counter-balance will create good co-ordination.

Strength and Power Exercises for Running

It may seem unlikely, but distance runners often have weak leg muscles. This is because, with a concentration on pure distance running, there is rarely time made during training for speed, power and strength work. However, it is absolutely necessary that speed and strength training is undertaken (see Chapter 14, Running Training). Exercises for strength and power are given below. Caution should be exercised, particularly if similar power training has not been done previously. Injury is possible if the exercises are hurried or are not performed properly.

Two Foot Explosive Jumps

Rebound (on both feet together) very lightly on the spot, then explode into bringing both knees up towards your chest. Go back to rebounding, then repeat the explosive effort, this time with two explosive efforts. Repeat up to ten counts, or until you are tired. Arms must be there for balance and upward lift.

Single Foot Explosive Jumps

This is the same as the previous exercise, but performed on one leg. This is extremely fatiguing and should only be undertaken by strong, experienced athletes.

Hopping

Following on from the above exercise, there are a number of hopping exercises that will promote strength and power.

Fast hopping with the strike over the mid-foot or ball of the foot will promote strength and power. Always attempt to keep an upright posture with the hips forward. Variations include:

- single foot hopping only;
- alternating three hops on one foot going on to three on the other foot;
- alternating two hops and one stride (sometimes called Indian hopping);
- alternating skipping and hopping.

The Running Ladder or Running Squares

The running ladder can be an unfolded rope ladder on the floor, or a taped line of squares. The athlete aims to run a series of drills, placing the foot in each square. Leg speed is focused on here, and the drills above used (a focus on fast leg speed and strength exercises). The running ladder is particularly helpful with new runners and triathletes and those who have initial problems with co-ordination.

The loneliness of leading the race. © *Nigel Farrow*

CHAPTER 10

TRANSITION

The Fourth Discipline

The 'fourth discipline' is the term used for the two changeovers in discipline, from swimming to cycling, and then from cycling to running. During a race, the changeover takes place in the transition area. All clothing and equipment other than that being used by the athlete has to remain here. The changeover is called the transition. The first transition from swim to cycle is sometimes called T1, and the second transition from bike to run, T2.

As triathlon is a continuous event (the clock doesn't stop between disciplines), the importance of a quick transition is obvious. Experienced triathletes will have taken part in transitions for every race in which they have competed, but for the inexperienced triathlete an enormous amount of time can be saved by practising and training for transitions.

Swimming uses the muscles in the upper body, cycling and running use the leg muscles and lower body. Blood will go to where it is needed; during the changeover from swimming to cycling the blood has to move from upper body to lower body muscles and there will be an initial feeling of emptiness.

Although cycling and running are both lower body activities, the legs will already be tired from cycling and this fatigue will be carried into the run. Ensure that you train correctly to be able to overcome this feeling. In addition, running is an impact exercise while the circular motion of pedalling is not. This impact may feel very strange in the early stages of the run (see Chapter 15, Back-to-Back Training).

Speed, Amount, Order

In the transition from swimming to cycling, wetsuits, swim hat and goggles have to be removed and a choice made as to whether the swimming costume will be worn during the cycle and run disciplines. Before taking hold of the bike and going out of the transition area, cycle clothing (shorts and top), crash hat and cycle shoes have to be put on, and the race number has to be placed correctly on the clothing (normally on the back of the top). Choices also have to be made about sunglasses and what is appropriate clothing for the weather. In the transition from cycling to running, the cycle clothing has to be removed and running shoes and clothing put on, as well as negotiating the bike into the transition area without crashing.

The importance of three things becomes immediately apparent:

- the speed of removing and putting on clothes;
- the amount of clothing to be worn;
- the order of undressing and dressing.

Clothing and equipment will not be located and changed quickly if it is set out in a haphazard order. Use the written checklist to ensure that the order of putting on clothing is reflected in the way that it is set out. If a number belt is not being used then time will be saved by having the race number already in place on the racing top. (Numbers can be worn under the wetsuit if in place on race clothing.)

It is crucial that the technique of transition is scheduled into a training programme, particularly in the early, learning stages. A mental checklist is important and although this mental list will become second nature with experience, it may

The fourth discipline, transition. © Nigel Farrow

The swim to cycle in action. © Nigel Farrow

be worthwhile writing down your own personal preferences of order of transition in the beginning stages. Experienced triathletes take a pride in having fast transitions, and at professional levels this may make the difference between winners and also-rans.

The technique of transition is as important as having excellent technique in the three disciplines, and as with the three disciplines, the skill is in maintaining that technique under pressure. The pressure often experienced during transitions can be the disorientation felt when surrounded by other triathletes, coupled with the exertion from the discipline just completed. Minutes rather than seconds can be saved in the early days.

Less is More

The rules governing clothing state that the top of the body (as well as the bottom) must be covered. Race rules also state that public nudity is forbidden, and although a blind eye is often turned, it is advisable to cover up if you are changing clothing in the transition area. These rules, however, give a great choice of what to wear and as time

is of the essence, going through the whole race without changing clothes will save a lot of time. It is entirely possible not to have to change clothing at all: wear in the swim, under the wetsuit, what you intend to wear during the entire race: a swimming costume or a tri-suit are both suitable. While male triathletes will need to have a vest or T-shirt, these can be worn under the wetsuit. Female triathletes will already have their tops covered and, if the water is too warm for wetsuits, then men have only to put a top on. Vests are usually easier than T-shirts as they don't have sleeves.

In the longer events, it may be worthwhile changing to specialist cycling and running clothing as the extra comfort will compensate for the extra time taken during transition. Many long-distance triathletes will choose to take a few extra seconds to put on socks for the running discipline.

Important Transition Points for Racing

Most transition areas operate a 'one way' system to minimize the chances of collision between triathletes, and it is essential to

know how this operates. There may be just one entrance/exit, or there may be one entry and one exit. For big events, there may be separate entrances and exits for swim, bike and run. Again, it is essential to locate these before the race starts. Cycling is never allowed inside the transition area for safety reasons. There is a mount and dismount line just outside transition (usually a painted or taped line on the road). This will be marshalled by race officials advising when you can mount and when you must dismount. Cycling crash-hats must always be fully on the head and secured before removing the bike from the racking where it will be located. In large events, there can be over a thousand competitors. Although not all competitors will start at the same time, it is important to know exactly where your bike is racked. This may sound self-evident but the disorientation experienced when coming out of the swim may make things appear different.

Sequence of Transition: Swim to Bike

From the swim finish approaching transition area

1   Start to loosen/take off goggles and swim hat, keep goggles and hat on forehead and head so you know where they are.
2   Place hand behind shoulder and undo the Velcro, then pull wetsuit zip halfway down.
3   Take your hand away from shoulder and put it behind your back and pull down the wetsuit zip completely.
4   Place one hand on opposite shoulder, hold the wetsuit tight and pull down over the arm and hand.
5   Repeat this on other side.
6   Ensure wetsuit is rolled down to waist and hip level.

Approaching the Bike

1   Put both hands on the wetsuit and pull down past the hips and down to below the knees.

This sequence shows the transition from the end of the swim into the run up to the bike.

The final wetsuit removal before the bike.

2   When most of the wetsuit is on the ground, put each foot in turn on the wetsuit and lift the other leg and foot high to roll down the remainder of the wetsuit.

3   Use hands and fingers to remove last of wetsuit from ankles and feet.

4   Take hat and goggles away from forehead and place on ground.

Before Taking Bike Out

1   If not already wearing a top under your wetsuit, put your cycle top on; if wearing a vest, it can be rolled inside out for easy putting on.

2   Check that your number is either pinned onto your top or vest or pinned to the elastic number belt.

3   Put on cycle shorts (if not already wearing them and if you are intending to wear them).

4   Put on cycle shoes unless you feel confident enough to have them already attached to the pedals.

5   Put on crash-hat and secure clasp.

6   If you are intending to wear sunglasses, place them into the top of your cycle top rather than wearing them immediately. It is highly likely that they will mist up at the start of the bike discipline because of the effects of the swim and the heat generated by your body at the start of the cycle.

7   Take your bike and run with it out of transition.

8   Mount your bike past the mount line; if your shoes are already attached to the pedals, run alongside your bike with hands on bottom of the handlebars and jump onto your bike.

9   Place feet inside shoes.

10   Start cycle discipline.

Sequence of Transition: Bike to Run

Approaching the finish of the bike discipline

1   Either undo the cycle shoes from pedals (clip out) or take feet out of cycle shoes and put feet on top of shoes while leaving them attached to the pedals.

2   Get off the bike immediately before the dismount line (if very crowded, you may save time by dismounting a little earlier).

3   Run with your bike to your allocated area within transition.

4   At allocated place in transition area place your bike on the bike rack.

5   Take off cycling shoes (unless they are clipped into the pedals and already off).

6   Unfasten crash-hat.

7   Take off crash-hat.

8   Take off cycle shorts and put on running shorts (if changing kit).

9   Decide whether to wear sunglasses.

10   Put on running shoes (unless you cycled in running shoes).

11   Exit transition and start run discipline.

Faster Transitions

If you wear less, there are fewer changes and this makes for a faster transition time. Here are some more tips.

•   Use a little Vaseline on the bottom of the legs and arms of the wetsuit, making it easier to put on and take off.

•   Use Vaseline or talcum powder on your cycling and running shoes.

•   Practise getting onto your bike with the cycling shoes already attached to the pedals. This will necessarily take a lot of practise and training but will save a great deal of time (see below).

•   Place your crash-hat upside down on your handlebars with the front of the

This sequence shows the transition from arriving at bike place to exiting transition. Note shoes attached to pedals, and bare feet.

Bike to run transition.

crash-hat towards you. It will save a few seconds.
- Use lacelocks, Velcro or elastic laces on your cycling and running shoes. Tying laces wastes time.
- Attached cycling shoes
- Place the pedals and cranks parallel to the ground in a flat position. Use elastic bands (they will snap as you

start to pedal) or Blu-Tack to keep them in position.
- Don't look down at your feet when putting them into the cycle shoes.

When you start to cycle, get some speed up before placing your feet inside the shoes, if you are riding too slowly and

looking down at your feet, you may fall off. (Some triathletes will choose to do the cycle section in running shoes if it is a short event. Make sure that you have the correct pedals for this option.)

There is no doubt that transitions can be difficult. However, it is part of the sport of triathlon and must be trained for appropriately.

PART 3

TRAINING

CHAPTER 11

PRINCIPLES OF TRAINING

The Unique Requirements of Triathlon Training

There are long-established, basic principles of training that will apply to most, if not all, sports. The beauty of triathlon is that these basic principles must take into account not only that three different endurance sports are being trained for, but also that each discipline will have an effect on the other two. When athletes come from one individual discipline into triathlon, the temptation will be to use the training used for that discipline and just transfer it into the other disciplines. That way lies disaster!

The different amounts of time and the different intensities of training that can be undertaken in the three sports are very different. As examples, it would not be at all unusual for a club cyclist to ride for four hours twice each week as part of their endurance training. If a runner (apart from the ultra distance marathon runners with many years of experience) were to attempt to run continuously for four hours twice each week then muscle soreness, injury, collapse and stress fractures would be the likely outcome, all this apart from extreme fatigue that would make training extremely difficult the following day. A 14-year-old club swimmer might well swim 20 repetitions of 200m with a recovery of between 10 and 30 seconds between each repetition during an ordinary club swimming training session at various times of the year. This might take between 60 and 80 minutes. If we translated that in terms of time into a runner's training schedule, it would equate to 20 repetitions of 800m (a rule of thumb to convert swim distances to run

distances is multiplying by four) and the 14-year-old would be carried away from the track. Many club swimmers are in the water training for 12 hours or more each week, and are able to handle this amount of training time, with the emphasis on interval and repetition-type training. Twelve hours of running interval training would be totally inappropriate for a young teenager.

The principles of training are fine but must be treated with caution by athletes and coaches entering triathlon from an individual discipline.

Triathlon training schedules must suit the individual and it is essential to look at the individual athlete in a number of important points:

- their age;
- their background sport and history, including any previous injuries;
- their strong and weak points;
- their reasons for taking up triathlon, aims and ambitions;
- the amount of time set aside each week to train.

All training is about adapting to change (a main training principle). Another way of considering this is that the body is dealing with the stress of training: too much stress and the body will not be able to deal with it, too little stress and improvements will not be sufficient or acceptable to the athlete. When stress (and training) is maintained at the correct levels, then progression and adaptation will take place; so appropriate training leads to appropriate adaptation. As adaptation takes place, the training stimulus becomes higher and further adaptation to a higher level of fitness takes place.

Basic Training Principles

None of the principles of training stands alone. They are closely inter-related and depend on each other. Most athletes and coaches would agree that the fundamental principles of training are included in this list.

- Individuality
- Adaptation
- Overload
- Progression
- Specificity
- Overtraining
- Rest and Recovery
- Reversibility
- Technique
- Mental attitude
- Physical limitations

Individuality

As discussed above, every athlete is an individual. General principles are fine, but each individual has their own specific needs and requirements. All athletes will respond in their own individual way to training.

Adaptation

Adaptation is the change the body makes in response to the training stimulus. Adaptation may occur in the short term, but importantly it is that adaptation over the long term that is crucial. If demands are progressive, adaptation will take place and will also be progressive. Too many demands too early will lead to a failing response. The body is continually broken down from training, and becomes stronger and fitter through the rest and recovery afterwards. Training is a process of:

- training (physical effort);
- breakdown;
- recovery;
- compensation and adaptation.

Once this process has occurred, the cycle will start again and gradually move up the circle of adaptation and increased fitness.

Overload

Training has to be sufficiently demanding to make the body adapt and so improve fitness and performance. The overload will depend on frequency of training, the length of each training session, and the amount and intensity of training done within each session. It is important to remember that as three disciplines are being trained, the body may not initially feel tired when starting training in a different discipline. However, that fatigue will eventually accumulate.

Progression

Distance, time and intensity of training will gradually become greater over a period of time as the athlete improves. This progression must necessarily be gradual if the athlete is to avoid injury, over-tiredness, disillusionment and boredom. Training will increase as the individual adapts to previous training loads. It is important to schedule in a short period of recovery training before progressing to more demanding training; this is often called the 'maintenance effect'. Fitness will not be lost overnight.

There will sometimes be periods of little or no improvement or even a decrease in performance. This is time for the body to adjust; this settling-in period is necessary for the body to adapt to its current level of training. A decrease in performance is often called the 'staircase effect'.

Overtraining

Following a hard training session, a hard week, a hard month or a hard season your body has been overtrained and will require a minimum time to recover. If training starts again before recovery is complete then levels of endurance, strength, speed and energy will all be low. Training at this time is not advised as it will lead to poor performance and extreme fatigue. Recovery is essential for long-term gains.

Specificity

The effects of training are specific to the individual triathlete, the type of training being undertaken, and the particular discipline. Individual triathletes need individual training plans to achieve maximum benefit. Fitting training around a club or squad means that some athletes will be training harder, some easier than others. Always be aware of the individual effect along with the specific effect. Although triathlon is largely an aerobic activity and there will be some crossover between the three disciplines on a general aerobic–cardiovascular level, specific gains in swimming will only be made by swimming training, similarly in cycling and running.

Rest and Recovery

Recovery is a most important part of the training programme, for it is during the

Don't forget, recovery is essential.

recovery phase after training is completed that adaptation takes place. Rest and recovery are closely linked with over-training (see above) and a combination of overtraining and insufficient recovery time is sure to slow down progress, if not stop it altogether. It is easy for individuals to ignore this point, believing that it is mental strength and attitude that carry them through the feelings of extreme fatigue. Sooner or later, it will catch up with them.

Full time professional triathletes have to treat training as their occupation and will ensure that they make time for rest and recovery every day. They will sleep during the day to ensure recovery from one training session to the next.

It is important to realize the different levels of stress that the body will endure. The continual jarring and impact of running training tends to make it the most difficult to recover from. Running on more forgiving surfaces such as grass and wearing good quality running shoes will lessen the effects but running is still more stressful than cycling and swimming and will need the most recovery time. Individual training backgrounds and entry fitness will also impact on recovery time. The type of training will have a strong input on recovery. An intense interval or repetition session will need more recovery time than an aerobic-based session such as a long, easy bike ride or a long, easy run on grass. As with most aspects of training, the amount of recovery will very much depend on the individual. As fitness increases, recovery time may be less.

One good measure of recovery is the heart rate. Although resting and maximum heart rates will vary between individuals, the recovery of heart rates (how quickly they return to normal after training) will give a good indication of fitness and indicate when to return to training.

Reversibility

Fitness depends on training, and if regular training ceases then the body will return to its previous state. Once again, the principle of individuality is important and the loss of fitness will vary between athletes. As a general rule of thumb, triathletes who have trained for a long time will lose their fitness more slowly than relative newcomers to training.

Technique

The importance of ensuring good technique cannot be over-emphasized. If skill is defined as 'maintaining technique under pressure' then maintaining that excellent technique through demanding training sessions and races is crucial. Triathletes should aim for excellent technique when training in all three disciplines to ensure that their technique stays constant during races.

Mental Attitude

Mental strength is vitally important for everybody. Without that mental toughness, every single training session can be a struggle. Without the mental strength to overcome setbacks, no one can fulfil their potential.

Physical Limitations

The first rule for being a successful athlete in any area of sport is to have chosen your parents wisely! Our genetic inheritance will play a major part in our physical (and mental) abilities – and our physical limitations. Whatever physical limitations we have, a strong mental attitude will go a long way to determining how much of that physical ability is used.

Types of Training

In the history of most sports particular types of training have been the most popular at certain times. Van Aaken's principle of training 'long distances, slowly,' contrasts vividly with Gershler's ideas on interval training, but there have been very successful runners using both methods. Not every type of training will work for

> **TOP TIP**
>
> Always remember, 'train to your weaknesses, race to your strengths'.

each individual, so it is important to know what types of training there are and what effects each will have on the body. The three disciplines of triathlon will all make use of the following outlines of training at some time.

- Overdistance training
- Distance training
- Race pace, tempo and time trials
- Interval and repetition training
- Fartlek
- Resistance training
- Technique
- Strength, speed and power training

It is important to see what each of the above training methods contributes. New triathletes enter the sport from a wide variety of backgrounds, many from one of the three contributing disciplines, but also many from other sports, or indeed, little sporting background at all. New triathletes will tend to be strongest at their background sport and the first consideration should be to work harder on the other two disciplines. Time allocated to training should reflect this.

Before training, it is important to establish a number of goals. A number of questions should be asked. What exactly is the goal or aim? How much time is available for training? What is the current state of fitness in each discipline?

Evaluate progress. Do I have a race to aim for? How many races will I compete in?

Overdistance and Distance Training

'Overdistance' describes any distance run that is longer than the race distance. Overdistance and distance training is required to set a basic aerobic level of fitness before the more intense types of

Distance work is an integral part of all triathlon training. © *Nigel Farrow*

training start. Endurance training is the ability to withstand physical stress over a prolonged period of time, and it is essential not to rush or to skip this fundamental aspect of training. The intensity of this type of training is fairly low, and also gives scope to work on technique in the early stages. Distance work is basic conditioning work and builds confidence and mental strength. Overdistance training will also help to teach the body to burn fat as a fuel as well as carbohydrate.

An Olympic distance triathlon takes as long as running a full marathon, and the correct distance training will reflect that amount of time. This endurance training can be over as much as double the distance of the discipline during the event.

Race Pace, Tempo and Time Trials

Attempting to swim, cycle or run at race speed for a shorter amount of time than race distance is a most important aspect of training. This tempo-type training is hard and is often neglected by triathletes. It is a basic need for training. If the speed required during a race is not practised during training, how can it be utilized in a race? These are the times and distances that may be used:

- swimming, a 400m time trial or a 10- or 15-minute swim for distance;
- cycling, a 10- or 25-mile time trial, or a 20-minute sustained effort on a turbo trainer (see Chapter 8, Cycling).
- running, a 5k road race or a 15- or 20-minute sustained effort for distance.

Interval and Repetition Training

Interval training and repetition training are often confused, or are considered the same. This is not true, and although there is no rigid division, interval training usually has a fairly short rest between the efforts while repetition training will have a longer recovery time but faster efforts (see below). 'Interval' refers to the time between efforts, not the efforts themselves.

An example of an **interval** running training session would be:

12 × 400m run in 80 seconds with 30 seconds recovery between each effort.

An example of a **repetition** running training session would be:

4 × 400m run in 65 seconds with 6 minutes recovery between each effort.

Many coaches, in running particularly, refer to the DIRT principle. In essence, interval training is made up of four factors:

1 The **D**istance of each run, swim or cycle;

Technique is everything! © Nigel Farrow

2   The rest **I**nterval between each run, swim or cycle;
3   The number of **R**epetitions of each run, swim or cycle;
4   The amount of **T**ime that each run, swim or cycle takes.

Applying this dirt principle to the first example above gives:

- Distance 400m
- Interval 30 seconds
- Repetitions 12 times
- Time 80 seconds.

Fartlek

Coming from the Scandinavian word (loosely) meaning 'speedplay', this is essentially a non-structured interval session with fast and easy periods of running, swimming or cycling. Although the strict DIRT factors are missing, this can be a very constructive group session when organized or led by a coach.

Resistance (and Strength) Training

Adding resistance makes training more difficult. This should not be done all the time, but specific use of resistance in training is extremely beneficial. Examples include:

- running and cycling up hills (hill training);
- using a big gear for cycling;
- swimming with hand paddles and T-shirts;
- tying the ankles together in swimming so that body position will become lower and more resistant to the water flow.

Technique

Excellent technique is essential and correct technique should be emphasized in every training session, not only at specific 'technique' sessions. Many coaches say that excellent technique is about overcoming resistance.

- A flat horizontal body position in swimming is essential to minimize water flow resistance.
- Good body position in cycling overcomes wind resistance while overall position must be examined in relation to bike set-up, gearing, cadence and pedalling.

- Running is the final discipline in a race and the onset of fatigue makes good technique even more essential.

(For more on technique, see Chapters 7, 8 and 9 on Swimming, Cycling and Running.)

Strength

Strength was discussed in the Resistance (and Strength) section above by integrating them into general training sessions. Having muscular strength may also make you feel more confident in challenging situations. Some triathletes may need more specific sessions if they feel they are muscularly weak in one discipline. Swimmers are very strong in the upper body, similarly cyclists in their lower body and legs.

Speed

Triathlon is an endurance event. So, too, are the marathon, the 10k open water swim and cycling's 100-mile time trial. However, whatever the distance, the event is won by the fastest athlete showing the best tactical awareness. Always include speed training in your training schedule.

Power

Power may not seem very relevant to triathlon, but being able to sprint away from another competitor and establish some physical distance between you can be important. Swimming away from another competitor by sprinting around a turning buoy, accelerating into and around a corner on the bike or making a fast break on a hill climb, or having the ability to sprint the final 200m of the run are all important.

CHAPTER 12

SWIMMING TRAINING

The importance of excellent technique in swimming has been discussed in Chapter 7. A small improvement in skill level will result in a big improvement in performance so the emphasis in training sessions should always be on technique. This is particularly so in triathlon because:

- triathletes will often come from a non-swimming background and improvements will be limited without improvement in technique,
- the distances for triathlon competition are usually comparable to the middle-distance and distance events (400m, 750/800m, 1500m and then for triathlon, 1.2 miles and 2.4 miles for half Ironman and Ironman competition).

Along with practising technique, there must also be a structured training programme for improvement in fitness. For two triathletes with equal fitness, the one with the better swimming technique will win the swim discipline; for two triathletes with equal technical efficiency, the one with the better swimming fitness will win the swim discipline.

For swimming more than cycling or running, it is highly recommended to have the help of a coach. While it can be obvious to the athlete during cycling and running training what is being done, during swimming training it is far more difficult to see. A coach is able to point out immediately any faults and technique changes required.

Realistic Training

Top class swimmers will often be in the pool and training for twenty or more hours each week, covering in excess of 70,000 metres. Clearly this is impractical for triathletes, as all training has to be shared between the three disciplines. This is a case in which the philosophy of 'Train to your weakness and race to your strengths' must come into play. If swimming is a weakness initially, then more time must be allocated to swimming training. Similarly, if swimming is a strength, then preference should be given to cycling and running. It is also important to approach training and the time required realistically. Apart from professional athletes and people who have retired from work, everybody has calls on their time, either work or school or the usual everyday living commitments. Many triathletes will base their training around nine sessions each week, although this is a very wide generalization. If an athlete has similar fitness and ability in all three disciplines, this assumes three swimming sessions each week. Training will be fitted in before work, at lunchtimes, and after work. Many swimming pools are open early in the morning (often from 6am or even before) to both leisure swimming and organized club swimming sessions. Swimming sessions are usually of between one and two hours' duration. With the limited amount of time available, it is important to look carefully at specific needs for triathlon. Interval-type training is the basis for most swimming sessions, but within this, the other aspects and requirements can all be covered. The total time for even a one-hour session means that overdistance and distance training are covered. Technique has been discussed and can be used in the sample session. Resistance training is catered for by using paddles, fins, pull buoys and kickboards, and also drag trunks and occasionally T-shirts. Strength, speed and power training can be seen on several parts of the training session; often the build before the main set, but also with specific short efforts, often after the main set.

Swimming training is hard but sets the opening standard for triathlon. © Nigel Farrow

Race Pace, Tempo and Time Trials

It is essential that target times for repetition training are both realistic and challenging. Such targets can be established by using a timed swim to establish baselines of speed. The timed swim can be a 20-minute or 30-minute swim to check the total distance covered, or a 1500m or 2000m swim with the time logged. The longer times and distances are more usual for older triathletes and swimmers. Careful analysis of these times and distances will allow triathletes and swimmers (and their coaches) to set specific repetition times for training, by measuring the present endurance levels indicated by the baseline swim for distance or time. By dividing the total time by the number of 100m swum, we can find our own baseline time for each 100m.

The target times would then be as follows:

- for 100m repetitions, multiply baseline 100m time by 96.5 per cent;
- for 200m repetitions, multiply baseline 100m time by 98.5 per cent;
- for 400m repetitions and above, use a straight division.

This 30-minute swim (with distance noted) can be used to retest to establish new targets.

A quick breakdown in the form of a checklist before setting out each training session would need to take into account some or all of the points in the box below.

The Training Session

In general, a swimming training session should contain all or most of the following features.

Warm-up

This can be as little as 10 per cent and as much as 25 per cent of the total training session depending on the emphasis of the session, time of year, and how the session relates to forthcoming competition or recovery from competition.

Build

A short series of repeat swims to prepare the athlete mentally, and the body physically, for training

Recovery swim

This is not always included. If it is, the focus is often on an aspect of technique and swimming drills.

Main set

This is the important part of hard physical training. It can vary between as little as 30 per cent and as much as 70 per cent of the total training session, again depending on the factors mentioned above.

Recovery swim

Again, this part of the training session usually concentrates on a technique or stroke.

Warm-down or swim-down

This comprises slower swimming, a reflection on the session and a chance for the body to relax.

Periodization

Swimmers will work on different aspects at different times of the year with the aim of coming into the major competitions rested and tapered and looking for personal best times on their races. For triathletes it is different. The distances are usually longer, up to 1500m or even longer, and there is a need to swim the 1500m distance as many as ten times a year during the triathlon racing season. There is a need for endurance training at all times and periods of training and each training session must reflect that.

Set out below are some sample swimming training sessions. Times are not indicated as, with the help of the 'timed swim' outline explained above, triathletes and coaches can establish their own repetition times.

Novice swimmers and triathletes may cover as little as 2000m during a one-hour training session. Experienced athletes may well double that.

	Type	Effort	Rest	Heart rate
Mixed aerobic	mixed strokes	comfortable	short	140–160
Endurance (main area for triathletes)	specific sets 6 × 400 or 10 × 200	hard, but able to maintain for 20–60 mins	short	160–180
Anaerobic	4 × 100 or 8 × 50	99 per cent	full recovery	max HR
Speed	16 × 10–20m	100 per cent		

Session One

Warm-up
- 400 front crawl full stroke: 200 front crawl, pulling (arms only, use a pull buoy), 400 full front crawl

Main set
- 20 × 50m with 15 seconds recovery between each swim

Warm-down
- 400m choice of stroke, 2 × 100 kicking (10 seconds between), 200 pull, 200 emphasizing long stroke
- Total distance 3000m

Session Two

Warm-up
- 200 front crawl, 200 pull, 200 full, 200 kick, 200 full front crawl

Main set
- 5 × 400m front crawl, recovery 30 seconds between

Warm-down
- 50 kick, 50 pull, 50 full × 4
- Total distance 3600m

Session Three

Warm-up
- 1000m straight swim: over-emphasize body roll and length of stroke

Main set
- 100m, 200m, 300m, 400m, 500m, 400m, 300m, 200m, 100m. Rest 15 seconds only between swims: 100m, 300m and 500m swims on full stroke, 200m and 400m swims on pulling

Warm-down
- 200m easy backstroke
- Total distance 3700m

Session Four

Warm-up
- 100m front crawl, 100m front crawl kick, 100m front crawl choice of drill, three times though

Main set
- 20 × 100m front crawl; rest 10 seconds only between swims

Warm-down
- 200m easy backstroke
- Total distance 3100m

Session Five

Warm-up
- 8 × 100m easy swim, 10 seconds between each. Attempt to lengthen stroke and body roll more on each successive 100m

Main set
- Three sets of 5 × 200m with a rest of 50, 40, 30, 20 and 10 seconds between each swim; repeat three times

Warm-down
- 200m easy swim on any other stroke
- Total distance 4000m

Session Six

Warm-up and build
- 8 × 50m, rest 5 seconds between each swim; then 3 × 100m with 10 seconds recovery, then 1 × 200m. Gradually increase speed and intensity, rest 10 seconds

Main set
- 3 × 800m, rest 1 minute between swims. First 800m full stroke, concentrate on long stroke and stroke count. Second 800m split at each 100m by 5 seconds, alternate 100m with full stroke and choice of drill. Third 800m split at each 200m by 10 seconds, alternate 200m, pulling and full stroke

Warm-down
- 4 × 200 easy pace. Recover 10 seconds between each 200m, with 50m each of kick, catch up, pull and full stroke (emphasizing body rotation)
- Total distance 4100m

Session Seven

Warm-up
- Continuous 800m. Breathe every three strokes

Main set
- 8 × 50m; recovery 10 seconds
- 4 × 100m; recovery 10 seconds
- 2 × 200m; recovery 15 seconds
- 1 × 400m; recovery 30 seconds
- 2 × 200m; recovery 15 seconds
- 4 × 100m; recovery 10 seconds
- 8 × 50m; recovery 10 seconds

Warm-down
- 400m easy pace; alternate front crawl and any other stroke each length
- Total distance 4000m

CHAPTER 13

CYCLING TRAINING

Choosing the Correct Gearing Ratio

The variable that cycling brings into the mix of training is the bike itself. There is no doubt that better equipment in cycling can make a bigger impact on performance than kit and equipment in swimming or running, but for the most part it is still efficient training that is the defining factor. The one extra variable in cycling is the gearing and the gear ratios. The

choice of gear and subsequent cadence is something that must be decided upon by the individual athlete, after considering their relative strengths and weaknesses. A strong, powerful athlete may choose to select a big gear with a lot of resistance while a smaller, lightly muscled athlete may choose to maintain a high cadence and a lower gear. Although history indicates that selecting a gear where the athlete can pedal at approximately 100rpm is the best trade-off between cadence and strength/power, this will not suit everyone.

Pedalling Efficiency

Pedalling is not a simple up-and-down action, and although the most power will be on the down push, it is important to bear in mind that the lifting (recovery) phase will be on the upstroke, and also the two possible dead-spots at the top and bottom of the pedalling action. On the upstroke it is necessary to pull the foot backwards at the end the downward stroke. The term sometimes used is 'ankling', with the toes pushed

Cycling is the longest discipline in distance and time, and this must be reflected in training. © *Nigel Farrow*

downwards and backwards. It is a similar action to attempting to scrape something off the shoe.

Pedalling with a single leg (use a turbo trainer, see Chapter 8) will demonstrate both dead-spots and also if there is a big difference in leg strength between left and right. Gradually increasing either the gear or cadence will help here as there will be a point where one leg will fail to cope more quickly than the other. Dead-spots will be revealed by single pedalling as it will appear that the chain has momentarily stopped or slowed when the dead-spot is reached. Dead-spots will occur at the top and bottom of the pedal action.

Evolution of Cycling Training

In some instances cycling training has evolved a little more slowly than training for either swimming or running. There has been considerable development in, and crossover between, swimming and running and the use of different varieties and types of interval training. However in cycling there has been a considerable history of several months away from training during the winter, long easy rides towards the end of winter and the beginning of spring, and then time-trials during spring. For many cyclists this worked, and if we examine this pattern more closely, we see that it follows one of our training principles: of building endurance before adding speed. More recently there has been more of a crossover between disciplines, and cyclists have learned to use interval and repetition training. However, in cycle training there has also been an increased use of Heart Rate Monitors (HRMs). Using this system, different levels of effort are required from the athlete and are monitored against heart rates (HR), having set the correct level by testing.

If this system is used, it is essential that testing is carried out. There are normally five levels of effort; level 1 being very easy and level 5 flat out speed. Although HRs must be set individually, the table below may explain a little more. Do not use these HRs as your own.

Heart rates are not necessarily the best accurate guide for level 5 intensity work. The training should rely more on perceived effort (RPE) with the HR being used and monitored for feedback. A week's training programme following these outlines might be similar to this:

> ### TESTING FOR MAXIMUM HEART RATE
>
> - Warm up until heart rate (HR) is constant.
> - Choose a gear where you can pedal at 95rpm for 2 minutes. Note HR at beginning and end of the 2 minutes.
> - Progress up through the gears every 2 minutes. Note HR at beginning and end of every 2 minutes.
> - Eventually the HR will level out after having risen constantly (although not necessarily consistently) throughout the test.
> - Now sprint until exhaustion.
> - Note down max HR as accurately as possible.
> - Warm down (spin) in easy gear and check HR recovery.

- **Monday** Recovery day
- **Tuesday** 35 sprints on turbo
- **Wednesday** 1 hour 45 minutes, level 3 ride
- **Thursday** Recovery day
- **Friday** 30 minutes continuous level 4 (either turbo or track)
- **Saturday** 3 hour level 2
- **Sunday** 4 hour level 2

Effort	Heart rate range	Purpose
Level 1	below 135bpm	Short rides for recovery Very long aerobic sessions
Level 2	135–165bpm	Development of economy and efficiency with high volume work. The wide zone is useful for long sessions but the majority of time should be spent below 155bpm
Level 3	155–165bpm	development of aerobic capacity with moderate volume work at a controlled intensity. This should normally be done alone or with a small group
Level 4	170–180bpm	Raising anaerobic threshold and acclimatization to race speed. This can be done (1) on a turbo; (2) for controlled periods within a shortened tempo session; (3) in a 10-mile or 25-mile time trial
Level 5	180bpm plus	High intensity interval training to increase maximum power and improve lactate tolerance. It is most conveniently and safely done on a turbo trainer

The cycle discipline is the longest in all triathlon events both in distance and time taken. It is important that enough base aerobic training is carried out before starting on the 'quality' and speed sessions set out below.

Negative Splits

One very useful training session to replicate the effort required during a race when fatigue sets in, is to ride out and back (perhaps with a very short break at the turnaround) but to attempt to return faster than going out. A 40k training ride might take 40 minutes outwards, a 2-minute break, and then aiming to complete the return in 38 minutes.

Turbo Training

It is often safer to train on the bike indoors. Using a turbo trainer (sometimes called a 'wind trainer') means that there is no need to worry about traffic or road conditions when doing a quality, interval-based training session. The turbo trainer also makes it easy to monitor progression in training. Most turbo trainers now have the facility to add extra resistance so making it easy to simulate hills even while training indoors.

Training Sessions Using Heart Rates

Lactate tolerance
- Warm up steadily to 80–85 per cent of maximum heart rate (MHR). Maintain this percentage for 40 minutes with rpm of 90–110. You will almost certainly need to change gears to maintain this heart rate.

Anaerobic threshold 1
- Warm up to 75 per cent of MHR.
- Ease back 10 beats per minute (bpm).
- Go into the large chainring and hold 100rpm until bpm reaches 85 per cent of MHR.

- Maintain this for 30 seconds.
- Change into the small ring until HR drops to 70 per cent of MHR.
- Repeat 10 times or until HR will not return to 70 per cent of MHR in less than 3 minutes.

Turbo Training Without Using Heart Rates

The following training sessions are based on progression, and also making use of that extra variable that we have in cycling, the gearing ratio (see Chapter 8 for explanation of gearing). Most bikes have an inner and an outer chainring; the number of teeth is smaller on the inner ring which allows double the number of gearing choices. For example, the outer ring may have 52 teeth, the inner ring 42 teeth. On the rear wheel are the gear sprockets which may number between six and ten. The sprocket nearest to the wheel will have the greatest number of teeth, the farthest sprocket from the wheel the least. The teeth on each succeeding sprocket will go up from (say) 13 to 15 to 17 to 21 to 23 up to perhaps 28 teeth.

Anaerobic threshold 2
There is also a basic anaerobic threshold training session that is ideal for the turbo trainer. It consists of a 6-minute effort at slightly faster than race pace for 20k or 40k; a 1-minute easy spin recovery, and then a repeat of the 6-minute effort for six repeats in total. Inexperienced triathletes and cyclists may wish to start with 4 × 4 minutes on the effort section and gradually increase the time and repetitions.

Resistance (Hill) Training

The important factor is increasing the time spent on each repetition despite the resting time remaining the same.

- Warm up
- Go into a 'difficult' gear where you can only maintain 80rpm or so (say 52 × 13); pedal flat out for 1 minute, out of the saddle.

- Recover for 1 minute in easy gear.
- Repeat in 52 × 13 for 2 minutes, recover for 1 minute.
- Repeat for 3, 4, 5 minutes.

Progressive (Increasing Demand) Cycling Training Sessions Using Gearing

The following training sessions are designed for the turbo trainer and for out on the road, but should only be carried out on the road if conditions are safe. It can be difficult to monitor heart rates, speed, cadence and power output while also checking road conditions. As discussed in Chapter 11, Principles of Training, it is not only the hard work time that is important but also the recovery time. The emphasis should be on restricting the time allowed for recovery, the 'interval' between efforts. Always warm up and warm down in training sessions using an easy gear to spin the legs.

Session 1
- 5 repetitions of 52 × 20 for 1 minute at 100rpm.
- Recovery: 42 × 20 for 1 minute at 60rpm.

First progression
- 10 repetitions of 52 × 20 for 1 minute at 100rpm.
- Recovery: 42 × 20 for 1 min at 60rpm.

Second progression
- 5 repetitions of 52 × 20 for 2 minutes at 100rpm.
- Recovery: 42 × 20 for 1 minute at 60rpm.

Third progression
- 7 repetitions of 52 × 18 for 2 minutes at 100rpm.
- Recovery: 42 × 18 for 1 minute at 60rpm.

Fourth progression
- 8 repetitions of 52 × 16 for 2 minutes at 100rpm.
- Recovery: 42 × 16 for 1 minute at 60rpm.

Fifth progression
- 15 repetitions of 52 × 18 for 1 minute at 100rpm.
- Recovery: 42 × 18 for 1 minute at 60rpm.

This progression continues by increasing number of repetitions, and/or time of the repetitions and/or increasing gears. If several progressions are missed, it might continue as follows.

Tenth progression
- 3 repetitions of : 52 × 20 for 2 minutes at 100rpm, straight into:
  - 52 × 18 for 2 minutes at 100rpm, straight into:
  - 52 × 16 for 1 minute at 100rpm.
- Recovery: 42 × 20 for 1 minute at 60rpm after each 5 minute effort.
- Another gap, and then

Further progression
- 12 repetitions of 52 × 16 for 1 minute at 100rpm.
- Recovery: 52 × 22 for 1 minute at 60rpm.

Further progression
- 3 repetitions of:
  - 52 × 20 for 4 minutes at 100rpm, straight into:
  - 52 × 18 for 3 minutes at 100rpm, straight into:
  - 52 × 16 for 2 minutes at 100rpm.
- Recovery: 42 × 20 for 1 minute at 60rpm after each 9 minute effort.

Further progression
- 2 repetitions of :
  - 52 × 22 for 2 minutes at 100rpm, straight into:
  - 52 × 20 for 2 minutes at 100rpm, straight into:
  - 52 × 18 for 2 minutes at 100rpm, straight into:
  - 52 × 16 for 2 minutes at 100rpm, straight into:
  - 52 × 15 for 2 minutes at 100rpm, straight into:
  - 52 × 14 for 2 minutes at 100rpm:

- Recovery: 42 × 22 for 2 min at 60rpm after first set of 12 mins effort.

Further progression
- 1 repetition of 52 × 20 for 4 minutes at 100rpm.
- Recovery: 52 × 22 for 1 minute at 60rpm.
- 1 repetition of 52 × 18 for 4 minutes at 100rpm.
- Recovery: 52 × 22 for 1 minute at 60rpm.
- 1 repetition of 52 × 17 for 4 minutes at 100rpm.
- Recovery: 52 × 22 for 1 minute at 60rpm.
- 1 repetition of 52 × 16 for 4 minutes at 100rpm.
- Recovery: 52 × 22 for 1 minute at 60rpm.
- 1 repetition of 52 × 15 for 4 minutes at 100rpm.
- Recovery: 52 × 22 for 1 minute at 60rpm.
- 1 repetition of 52 × 14 for 4 minutes at 100rpm.
- Recovery: 52 × 22 for 1 min at 60rpm.

This progression is simplified and may have more intermediate steps depending on athlete, and standard and ability. However the rationale is valid. There are literally hundreds of different combinations that can be used to make up turbo sessions. The above are examples of these.

Power and Sprint Training Sessions

Despite the need for distance and aerobic background before training on the interval-type sessions, there may be occasions when sheer power and sprinting ability are required.

Short sprints
Choose a big gear (perhaps 52 × 13) and sprint flat out for only 5 seconds. Recover for 10 seconds only and repeat the effort ten times.

Progressive training leads to progressive performance. © Nigel Farrow

- Warm up.
- Sprint flat out (big gear) for 5 seconds.
- Recover 10 seconds only.
- Repeat ten times.
- Easy recovery for 1 minute.
- Repeat all the above three further times, so that 40 × 5-second sprints are done in all.

Session 2, longer sprints
- Warm up and then select a gear which is slightly 'too big'.
- Sprint for 15 seconds.
- Recover until HR has dropped to approximately 70 per cent of maximum HR.
- Repeat five to ten times.

CHAPTER 14

RUNNING TRAINING

All new triathletes will have run at some time; whether they come from a running background or whether they have played a ball game of which running is an integral part. Running is natural activity that almost everyone, athlete or otherwise, has done at some time. However, running in a triathlon can be a different experience from 'pure' running. Of the three disciplines, running is the least complicated, but you have to run after having already swum and cycled. Initial experiences of running in a triathlon may be very different from previously experiences of running as a single sport. The circular motion of cycling and the blood pooling in the cycling muscles are not ideal immediately before a 5k or 10k run: the fatigue that is brought into a run may be severe.

Requirements

There are no short cuts in becoming a good triathlon runner in triathlon events. Technique, speed, strength and mobility training together with an awareness of the specific requirements of triathlon running will lead to longer and faster performances. In triathlon specifically, and in running generally, the following points are important and must be borne in mind when designing a training programme.

Triathlon is largely an aerobic activity, even in the shorter sprint and Olympic-distances events. Outstanding athletes will take one hour for a sprint event and two hours for an Olympic-distance event. These times are comparable to running a half-marathon (13.1 miles) or a full marathon (26.2 miles) compared to distances of 750m/1,500m swim, 20k/40k bike, and 5k/10k run. The term 'sprint distance' for an event lasting one hour is a misnomer. The majority of training should be endur-ance based. However, endurance training alone is not sufficient to run fast during a triathlon: running speed work has also to be done. This should not be done without sufficient endurance work. Running speed will be affected by leg strength, stride length and mobility, leg speed (cadence), type and amount of training and body weight.

Specificity

Running training must be specific to have maximum effect, therefore fatigue must be endured in training in order to cope with it in races. This is particularly relevant in a triathlon because the run is the final discipline. Low level (or general) fatigue can be endured; very high level fatigue may only be endured for a short time. In triathlon particularly, compensated fatigue is the tiredness in a training session that is carried over from previous training sessions. There will always be a point of failure if you go past current physical and mental limits; but by appropriate, progressive and specific training, those points of failure will be extended.

Improving running speed will make it easier to 'cruise' at a faster pace on longer distances. It is important to train at a pace and at speeds faster than race pace regardless of distance.

The amount of running training is important; however, equally important is the content of any training load. Training at one pace only will not lead to any significant improvements. Endurance running is important as a base upon which to build tempo and speed running. A solid endurance background established during the early period of training is essential. Attempting to miss this foundation period and go directly into speed running may lead to injury. What is then specifically done in the build-up to an important race will determine the level of success in that race. The amount of preparatory training before that build-up period will determine the amount and intensity of training in the period before the race.

Of the three disciplines, running training brings with it the most likelihood of injury. Every potential and minor injury should be regarded as if it might become a major one. Water or aqua running may go some way to help avoid injuries. Running is the only triathlon discipline in which our own bodyweight is carried and supported, and this bodyweight is quadrupled by the impact of running. This increases the likelihood of injury, with the resultant strains and stresses on the bones, tendons, muscles and joints of the legs, hips and feet. If injury does occur, it should be treated as a potential major injury; the appropriate advice should be sought and action taken.

Principles and Needs of Running Training

Adapting from the general principles of training, running training should comprise:

- steady running over short, medium or long distance;
- interval and repetition (including Fartlek);
- strength and resistance (hills) running;
- tempo and time train running (race pace);
- negative split running (coming back faster than outward);
- specific demands of triathlon running.

GOOD RUNNING TECHNIQUE
REQUIRES:

- a good oxygen uptake (efficient lungs) and the ability to use this uptake;
- a good anaerobic capacity (oxygen debt tolerance; the determination and ability to maintain fast running when the oxygen has been used up);
- the ability to run fast and the ability to maintain adequate speed over long distances (this may depend on the body's ability to easily use fat as a fuel as well as carbohydrate.

Endurance Progression

At the basic entry level, the need is to be able to run, and to be able to maintain running over the race distance. The first step is to run and to gradually build up endurance. It is crucial that progression in training (running for a longer amount of time each week) is built up gradually. A

Hill running is an integral part of training.

new runner or triathlete might follow a basic training schedule like the one below, assuming three runs each week.

- **Weeks One and Two**: three easy runs of 3 miles or 20 minutes
- **Weeks Three and Four**: two easy runs of 3 miles or 20 minutes, one run of 4 miles or 30 minutes
- **Weeks Five and Six**: two easy runs of 4 miles or 30 minutes, one run of 6 miles or 50 minutes
- **Weeks Seven and Eight**: two easy runs of 4 miles or 30 minutes, one run of 8 miles or 60 minutes.
- **Weeks Nine and Ten**: one easy run of 4 miles or 30 minutes, one run of 6 miles or 50 minutes, one run of 8 miles or 60 minutes.

It is important to state that the mileage and times given are not necessarily related; the progression can be in individual run and total run time, and also in individual run distance and total run distance. The progression above goes from 1 hour to 2 hours 20 minutes, and also from 9 to 18 miles (14–29km). The training load has been doubled in ten weeks, an excellent progression for a new triathlete.

Interval Running Progression

The importance of interval training in swimming, cycling and running was discussed earlier. It is as important to make realistic progressions in interval training as it is in endurance training. This can be summarized by the acronym DIRT, where **D** is **distance** run, **I** the **interval** of rest or recovery, **R** the number of **repetitions** to be run, and **T** the **time** that the distance of the run takes. For progression to be made in running training, these four factors can be adjusted:

- the **number** of repetitions can be increased;
- the **distance** of the repetitions can be increased;
- the **resting time** between the repetitions can be decreased;

- the **time taken for completing** the repetitions can be decreased.

A running training session might be four repetitions of 800m to be completed in 3 minutes each, with a resting interval of 3 minutes between each repetition.
  In training shorthand:

- 4 × 800m in 3 minutes, RI 3 minutes

First progression
- 5 × 800m in 3 minutes, RI 3 minutes

Second progression
- 5 × 800m in 3 minutes, RI 2 minutes 30 seconds

Third progression
- 5 × 800m in 2 minutes 45 seconds, RI 2 minutes 30 seconds

Fourth progression
- 5 × 1000m in 3 minutes 25 seconds (equivalent to a time of 2 minutes 45 seconds for 800m, RI 2 minutes 30 seconds).

Once these four progressions have been made, there is further improvement by once again increasing the number of repetitions from 5 × 1000m to 6 × 1000m, and so on.

Five Pace Training

The theory of five pace running is that running training should be done at:

- race pace;
- faster than race pace (in shorter distances in training);
- significantly faster than race pace (very short distances in training);
- slightly slower than race pace (for longer distances during training);
- an easy pace (when distance to be covered in training is long).

To improve speed and endurance, training needs to be carried out both faster and longer than the race distance. For an Olympic distance run in triathlon of

Running training in a group leads to higher standards. © *Nigel Farrow*

Session	Pace	Distance	Recovery
1		20km run (endurance)	
2	10k pace	3 × 3000m	90 seconds to 2 minutes recovery
3	steady run, faster than the pace for 20km	12 to 14km	
4	5k pace	3 × 2000m	with 90 seconds to 2 minutes recovery
5		15km run (endurance)	
6	3k pace	5 × 800m	with 90 seconds to 2 minutes recovery
7		20km run (endurance)	
8	1500m pace	6 × 600m	2 minutes to 2 minutes 30 seconds recovery
9	steady run	12 to 14km	
10	800m pace	16 × 200m	90 seconds to 2 minutes recovery
11		15km run (endurance)	
12	400m pace	8 × 100m at sprint pace	90 seconds to 2 minutes recovery

10 kilometres, speed sessions are required at faster than that pace (perhaps at 1500m and 800m pace), and endurance runs are required for longer than 10km (12 to 20km). As speed increases for the shorter distances, this, coupled with the endurance training, will ensure improvements over 10 kilometres. Athletes must do this on a regular basis. A sample running programme based on the five-pace theory is set out below.

Note that recovery time in relation to distance and effort is significantly more when the pace is fast and the distances shorter. It is preferable to jog during the recovery times rather than do nothing.

Specific 10-kilometre running training programme

Just as in swimming, it is possible to use a timed swim to set a programme for relative speeds, so it can be used in designing a running training programme.

The starting point is found by running for 15 minutes and measuring the exact distance covered, for example 3000m. A running track is ideal.

Then, six specific sessions should be used to maximize the potential of training. With the tempo run being done twice during the each phase of training, these six sessions largely conform to our five-pace running programme.

Run twice the set distance (6000m) in double the time plus 10 per cent or 3 minutes (33 minutes). Aim to reduce this by 1 minute every 6 weeks. This session should be done twice within each phase of training.

Run three repetitions of half the distance (1500m) in 7 minutes 30 seconds with 1 minute recovery between the efforts. More recovery time may be necessary initially. Aim to reduce the time or increase the distance by 15 seconds or 70m every 6 weeks.

Find your 400m pace from the timed run (2 minutes for each 400m.) Halve this (60 seconds) and take off another 8 seconds to find the correct 200m pace (52 seconds). Run a series of 200m in 52 seconds with reducing rest. Start at 90

seconds, then 75, 60, 45, 30, 15 seconds; start again at 90 seconds and keep going until you can't maintain 52-second pace.

Run more than the 10km distance. Start at 10km plus a third (13 kilometres) and gradually work up to double the distance (20km). This is a run for endurance, and speed is not an essential.

Hills, resistance and strength work come in this session. Either run 10km on a hilly course, with approximately half of the distance uphill, or run hill repetitions. Run fast uphill and jog down each time.

There are six training sessions in all before the programme is repeated. An athlete running three times each week will cover the six sessions in a two-week period. Re-testing should be done every six to eight weeks and the times adjusted.

If using the five-pace training programme, it is important to know comparative and equivalent speeds for the various distances. All those set out below are not always totally accurate with very fast or very slow runners; they are about 90 per cent accurate for the majority of athletes. The times and speeds are for men; women's times follow in the brackets.

Equivalent Times and Distances

- Using 1600m (one mile) to start: for athletes who have a 1500m time, work out the average pace for 100m, and add that for the 1600m time.
- To find your best 800m time, halve your 1600m (one mile) time and deduct 11 seconds (women 13 seconds).
- To find your best 400m time, halve your 800m time and deduct 5.5 seconds (women 6.5 seconds).
- To find your 3000m, add 20 seconds to your 1500m time and double it (women add 24 seconds).
- To find your 5000m time, multiply your 1600m time by 3 and add 2 minutes (women add 2 minutes 20 seconds).
- To find your best 10,000m time, double your 5000m time and add 75 seconds (women add 90 seconds).

These times will not stand up if insufficient training has been undertaken.

Other Factors for Running Training

- Running in a triathlon is mainly (80 per cent) aerobic. Ensure that adequate training is done at aerobic level and attempt to raise the aerobic threshold of training.
- Grass and soft surfaces are kinder to your legs than hard surfaces.
- Speed sessions at faster than racing pace are important.
- Some longer training runs should be tried for negative splits (run back faster than outwards).
- Regular resting and recovery weeks are essential.
- Train with athletes who are faster to raise standard and speed of running.
- Flexibility in the training programme is important.
- Always be aware of the possibility of injury from overtraining. An excess of speed work will often cause this.

Total exhaustion after total commitment.
© Nigel Farrow

CHAPTER 15

BRICK TRAINING, BACK-TO-BACK TRAINING, SPECIFIC TRIATHLON TRAINING

Although training in one discipline will not make you a better athlete in a different discipline, there are a number of benefits that carry over from training in one to another.

These are the benefits of training in all disciplines and all are linked together:

- Building and maintaining a good, strong overall aerobic base;
- Improved mobility and flexibility from training and using other muscles than would be required in a single sport;
- An avoidance of overuse injury;
- Avoidance of boredom;
- Development of strong antagonistic muscles.

Aerobic Effect

All endurance sports require aerobic training; swimming, cycling and running will increase the amount of oxygen getting from the lungs to the working muscles. Only active muscles will be affected, so muscular transfer between disciplines is very restricted, and only muscles that are used in more than one activity will receive any benefit. There is a little transfer of muscle use between cycling and running. However, aerobic training has a similar training effect on similar types of muscle fibres; endurance training stimulates the slow-twitch fibres and the efficiency of these will improve whatever the aerobic training method used.

Mobility and Flexibility

Single discipline specialists repeatedly use the specific muscles and joints employed in that sport. Unless they are very disciplined and have a comprehensive mobility training plan, a loss of flexibility is likely. Multidiscipline triathletes will get the benefits of extra flexibility by exercising muscle groups which a single sport exponent would not use.

Injury

Athletes training hard for long periods of time are always at risk of overuse injury. As time has to be made for all three contributing disciplines in triathlon, the risk of injury is likely to be less. However, if injury does occur in one discipline then training can often be continued in the other two disciplines.

Agonist and Antagonist Muscles

Muscle movements are undertaken by the **agonist** muscles. These are shortening movements. The **antagonist** muscles are those that lengthen and balance the movement. Antagonist muscles are frequently not strong enough to balance the agonist muscles. In triathlon it is more likely that they will balance.

Back-to-Back and Brick Training

As triathlon is a sport where the three disciplines follow each other with no break, it makes sense to train in this manner as well. When one discipline is immediately followed by another discipline in training, this is called **back-to-back** training; when there are more than two elements, perhaps bike-to-run-to-bike-to-run, this is referred to as **brick training**. In practice, these terms are largely interchangeable. This type of training is very demanding and tiring and adequate recovery time should be scheduled after a back-to-back training session. In the early stages of competing, changing from one discipline to the next is difficult. With experience it becomes less so and this should be reflected in training.

'Bricks' helps your body get used to going immediately into the next event. You not only gain a physiological benefit but also gain a mental preparation for a race. When racing, things will feel more familiar and you will have an edge on those who fail to practise for race conditions.

In particular, brick training teaches you how to run fast and efficiently when you come off the bike by monitoring output on the bike phase and adjusting it so that you do not carry too much fatigue into the run. This may mean developing better cycling technique. Triathlon brick training is perfect for testing this out.

The normal order in a triathlon is swim to cycle to run. Back-to-back training sessions are most commonly bike to run, or less commonly swim to bike, so as to adapt to the race situation. As with any training session, the focus can be one factor or more. It is not necessary to focus only on endurance. The need for speed when already tired from a previous discipline should also be addressed.

Swim to Cycle

Swimming exercises predominantly the upper body and arms; cycling mainly the lower body and legs. Naturally blood will

Back-to-back and brick training make the transition during a race that much easier.
© Nigel Farrow

- A fast swim followed immediately by a fast cycle. This simulates race conditions. It is extremely demanding and should not be used too frequently in training. There are other more specific training sessions that we will examine later in this chapter.

Cycle to Run

Cycle to run training is considered more demanding than that from swim to cycle. The legs are already fatigued from cycling and then they have to run. Training for this changeover is essential in the early days of triathlon training. The ability to run well during a triathlon race is related not only to the athlete's running ability, but also and more so to the ability to cope with accumulated fatigue and pain.

Examples of Bike to Run Training Sessions

Standard training sessions:

- A steady ride of 10, 20, or 40 kilometres followed immediately by running 3, 5, or 10 kilometres. As with the swim to cycle, this training session simulates exactly what is required during a race. It is a basic session that should be used in the early stages of training.
- A hard ride followed immediately by a steady run. This simulates the sensation of a hard cycle discipline and then having to maintain concentration on the run when the legs are extremely fatigued.
- A steady ride followed immediately by a fast run. This simulates having to increase the run pace.
- A fast cycle followed immediately by a fast run. This simulates race conditions. It is extremely demanding and should not be used too frequently in training. As with the swim to bike training, more specific training sessions will follow in this chapter.

go to where it is required. Training for the swim to cycle prepares the body for the blood to be redirected to the legs after swimming.

Examples of Swim to Bike Training Sessions

Standard training sessions:

- A steady swim of 400m, 800m or 1500m followed immediately by riding 10, 20, or 40 kilometres. This

training session simulates exactly what is required during a race. It is a basic session that should be used in the early stages of training.

- A flat-out swim followed immediately by a steady cycle ride. This simulates the sensation of a hard swim and then having to maintain concentration onto the cycle discipline when already fatigued.
- A steady swim followed immediately by a fast cycle ride. This simulates having to increase the pace if necessary.

Endurance Back-to-Back and Brick Training Sessions

Training for longer time and distance than racing distance will build endurance. For Olympic distance racing (1500m swim, 40km bike and 10km run), these training sessions would be considered as endurance sessions.

Back-to-Back Sessions

- A 2km swim followed by 60km ride
- A 60km or two-hour ride followed by a 12km or one-hour run

Brick Sessions

- An 800m swim followed by 20km ride repeated twice more for total distances of 2,400m swim and 60km ride.

Swim to Bike Specific Session

It is logistically good to use a turbo trainer for both the swim to bike training and for bike to run training sessions. If it is possible to set up a turbo trainer on the poolside or in a changing room, it will make training easier.

Warm up as you would for a race, then:

- Swim 400m at race pace;
- Change into cycle shoes and change clothes only into what you intend to wear during a race;
- Cycle on turbo (or on nearby road circuit if no access to a turbo) for 8 to 12 minutes at race pace or slightly faster;
- Take 5 minutes' break and recovery and repeat four further times.

Bike to Run Specific Session

This training session can be done at any time of the year. The example given below is for pre- or early season for simulation of race demands. Training more slowly and with little rest would be an endurance session.

This session is very specific, attempting to run faster on each repetition despite being more fatigued each time. Once again, using a turbo trainer makes the session more practicable.

Warm up, then:

- 5km cycle in 8 minutes, then fast transition immediately into
- 1000m run at race pace. Recover for 5 minutes.
- Repeat 5k cycle in 8 minutes, then run 1000m faster than before. Recover for 5 minutes.
- Repeat 5k cycle in 8 minutes, then run 1000m faster than first repetition. Recover for 5 minutes.
- Repeat 5k cycle in 8 minutes, then run 1000m faster than second repetition. Recover for 5 minutes.
- Repeat 5k cycle in 8 minutes, then run 1000m faster than third repetition. Recover fully.

It is important to maintain good running technique and a fast cadence during this session.

Specific Triathlon Training Sessions

Although these are not brick training sessions but single discipline training sessions, they are aimed specifically at the demands of triathlon rather than those of each individual sport.

Swim

Triathlon swimming has two requirements in addition to the fast swimming needed in the single sport. First, the ability to 'draft off' another swimmer, staying close so the swimmer in front is doing the hard work; second, the ability to swim very fast at the start so as to take advantage of the drafting effect from faster swimmers. It is evident that a fast start will enable efficient drafting. It is important to simulate that flat-out start in training.

Triathlon Swim Specific Session

This swimming session simulates the explosive start and then the maintaining of race pace when you are extremely tired from those early efforts.

- Swim 100m flat out, rest 10 seconds only
- Swim 100m at race pace, rest 30 seconds
- Swim 100m flat out, rest 10 seconds only
- Swim 200m at race pace, rest 30 seconds
- Swim 100m flat out, rest 10 seconds only
- Swim 300m at race pace, rest 30 seconds
- Swim 100m flat out, rest 10 seconds only
- Swim 400m at race pace, rest 30 seconds.

Run

Cumulative fatigue is a huge factor on the run during a triathlon race. It makes sense to simulate that fatigue during a training session. Decreasing the recovery time while maintaining speed will assist in this. It will help to have an idea of pace; see Chapter 9 for information on equivalent speeds for different distances.

Run, Maintaining Speed When Fatigued (1)

Warm up, then:

- Run 200m, recovery jog for 90 seconds
- Run 200m, recovery jog for 75 seconds
- Run 200m, recovery jog for 60 seconds

- Run 200m, recovery jog for 45 seconds
- Run 200m, recovery jog for 30 seconds
- Run 200m, recovery jog for 15 seconds; after this very short recovery
- Run 200m, recovery jog for 90 seconds and repeat the series of repetitions
- Repeat series of repetitions once more.

If the pace cannot be maintained through the session, attempt a slower pace next time. If pace is not sufficient to fatigue, attempt a faster pace next time.

Run, Maintaining Speed When Fatigued (2)

This triathlon running training session is important for increasing speed when fatigued or under pressure.

- Run 400m slightly faster than 5k racing pace
- Run 400m at 10k race pace. This is important: the recovery runs are no slower than 10km racing pace throughout the training session
- Run 300m slightly faster than 1500m race pace
- Run 300m at 10km race pace
- Run 200m slightly faster than 1500m race pace
- Run 200m at 10k race pace
- Run 100m fast
- Run 100m at 10km race pace
- Then repeat this sequence twice more.

The athlete runs faster as they become progressively more fatigued. It is essential that the recovery runs are no slower than 10km race pace.

It is important to emphasize again that back-to-back and brick training is physically very demanding. Always have sufficient recovery time between brick sessions.

Preparing for transition starts upon exit from the swim. © Nigel Farrow

CHAPTER 16

DIET AND NUTRITION

Apart from a very few elite events, there are no heats and finals in a triathlon, which is hardly surprising when you consider that a sprint race (half the standard Olympic distance) takes around an hour for top class athletes. This takes away the necessity of planning eating and drinking between races. However, it makes it even more important that good habits in nutrition and hydration are established for general training and racing.

The amount of training and its intensity are the critical ingredients in determining fitness, and although this fitness will not be significantly enhanced by a good diet, a poor diet will significantly lower that fitness. Proper fuelling will influence fitness and race performance. It is not only what

Proper nutrition is an important part of racing and training. © Nigel Farrow

you eat and drink that is important, but also when you eat and drink.

A healthy diet provides the body with energy. The correct racing weight and use of ergogenic aids (such as energy drinks) as well as a possible need to drink and eat during longer events also needs to be considered.

What is a Healthy Diet?

We live in a society where food is abundant. The variety and choice available to us in the Western world is unparalleled in history. However, this choice combined with influential advertising can easily confuse. There may be some need for special nutrition for the athlete but generally an ordinary healthy diet should be adequate. Too much sugar, salt and saturated fat will be detrimental, although no one should completely cut them out. Too much alcohol is detrimental too and can be eliminated.

There is a basic need for energy to fuel the body and an increase in the amount of calories will be necessary for somebody in hard training. New entrants to triathlon, or any endurance sport, will often lose a significant amount of weight (body fat) in the early days of training, and because triathlon is a weight bearing sport and activity, that weight loss in the early days will by itself lead to significant improvements in performance and training times. While the general non-active population may require between 2000 and 2500 calories each day, very active triathletes may double that requirement.

Carbohydrate is the main supplier of energy and triathletes may need as much as 60 per cent of their calorie intake from carbohydrates. As much as 20 per cent will come from quality protein and per-

haps 20 per cent from fat. Caution must be exercised when reading these figures as ideas and advice change often. It is also necessary to have sufficient vitamins, minerals and fluids.

Energy Systems

Food provides the fuel that is converted into energy. Carbohydrate is used first, then fat, and finally protein. However, none of these nutrients stand alone and some fat will be used along with carbohydrate and a minimal amount of protein. However, apart from a tiny amount, protein is only used as a fuel when the other sources are depleted. When this happens, it is a big warning sign that over-exertion is taking place.

Carbohydrate, fat and protein are converted into glucose, fatty acids and amino acids, and these are used by the body to give the necessary energy.

The glucose is stored in the muscles and liver as glycogen. The muscle glycogen is used as fuel (liver glycogen provides glucose to the brain). Although glycogen can be stored in the muscles and can increase with the effect of training, it is very limited, and will become depleted during a long race or in hard training. Fat will then be used as the energy supplier but it is not a very efficient energy releaser and most people will train at a lower intensity when fat becomes the energy provider. Experienced athletes with a long history of endurance training are able to convert the fat more quickly and efficiently.

As fat will be used more as a race progresses, the pace of most athletes will slow down when fat becomes the major energy provider. For the swim and the cycle elements, carbohydrate will be the major contributor, but later in the race –

usually during the run – a higher percentage of fat is used. Its inefficiency will often be demonstrated by the athlete slowing down considerably in the run discipline.

Carbohydrates

Carbohydrate foods consist of complex carbohydrates – cereals, grains and bread, porridge, pasta, rice etc. – and simple carbohydrates, such as sugar.

Carbohydrates provide the most energy and should form the basis of each meal. Most carbohydrate foods contain significant amounts of essential vitamins and minerals, and, in an unprocessed state, fibre.

Carbohydrates may be starches (complex carbohydrates) or sugars (simple carbohydrates). Generally, complex carbohydrates are preferable although when 'instant' energy is required, the simple carbohydrate comes into its own.

Because the body's and muscles' carbohydrate stores are quickly used, athletes should ensure that they eat very soon after competition and training, within 20 minutes if possible. This will ensure that recovery is faster and that competition performance is improved.

Even more importantly, drink plenty of water at all times.

Protein

Protein foods also contain essential vitamins and minerals and may serve as a source of energy if required. They consist of animal protein – meat, fish and chicken; milk, cheeses, yoghurt, eggs – and plant protein – grains, nuts and seeds.

Protein is essential for building and repairing body tissues. The continual stress that the body undergoes during intense training makes it essential that sufficient protein is taken in to repair and rebuild the body. However, as high protein foods can also be high in fat, care should be taken. Vegetable-based protein contains less fat than meat-based protein. High protein foods can also take longer to digest and can cause discomfort if the

triathlete is training more than once each day. Extra protein intake, which is unused, cannot be stored in the body and is simply excreted.

Fat

Fat is the most concentrated source of food energy. Each gram of fat supplies nine calories, (four for protein and carbohydrate). Good sources of fat are: butter, margarine, fatty meat, chicken skin, milk and cheese, ice-cream, nuts and seeds.

Cholesterol and Saturated Fats

Cholesterol is present in meat, poultry and fish, milk and eggs. There is no cholesterol in fruit and vegetables, grains, nuts, seeds and dried beans and peas. High blood cholesterol levels tend to increase the risk of heart disease, and saturated fats raise blood cholesterol levels. Saturated fat is in the fats of whole milk, cream, cheese, eggs, butter, meat and poultry. Saturated fats solidify at room temperature.

Monounsaturated fatty acids and polyunsaturated fatty acids may have a beneficial, lowering effect on blood cholesterol levels. All fats, whether they contain mainly saturated fatty acids, monounsaturated fatty acids, or polyunsaturated fatty acids, provide the same number of calories.

Fat can only be used as fuel aerobically (endurance based exercise) whereas carbohydrate can be utilized both with and without oxygen.

Vitamins and Minerals

The majority of triathletes do not require vitamin supplementation; however, it may benefit those on a very restricted diet of less than 1200 calories per day or those with very poor eating habits. In these cases, a low dose, broad range nutritional supplement may help. Vitamins are necessary for red blood cell formation, for using oxygen and for metabolizing carbohydrate, protein and fat. Minerals are an essential nutrient in the diet. Calcium is used in

neuromuscular activity, and iron in oxygen transport. Iron deficiency can often occur amongst endurance athletes (often, but not always in female athletes). If iron is low, there is less available for haemoglobin formation (haemoglobin is the substance in the blood essential for carrying oxygen around the body) and its concentration decreases. The oxygen-carrying capacity of the blood depends on haemoglobin concentration and low levels are associated with a decrease in maximum oxygen uptake and therefore in physical working capacity. Iron deficient (anaemic) individuals show symptoms of early fatigue, breathlessness and headaches. Supplements of minerals are generally not necessary for athletes eating a diet adequate in both quality and quantity.

Vitamins

Vitamins occur in many foods and are easily provided in a properly prepared mixed diet containing fresh fruits and vegetables.

Unless an athlete is deficient in vitamins, vitamin supplementation is not required. Only the fat-soluble vitamins (A, D, E and K) can be stored in the body (primarily in the liver), but a healthy triathlete eating a well-balanced diet will receive adequate amounts of all the essential vitamins. A vitamin deficiency may lower performance. A lack of the B vitamins normally has the most immediate effects, as does a lack of thiamine, while the effects of vitamin A deficiency may not appear for months. Care must be taken in cooking and preparing food as this may reduce the vitamin content (particularly vitamin C). Leaving the skin on fruit and vegetables and steaming or microwaving is better than frying.

Minerals

Minerals provide the substance for bones and teeth and are present in soft tissues and fluids allowing the cells to work properly. Mineral supplementation will not help performance unless there is a deficiency. A poor diet may lead to deficiencies in iron (see above) and zinc.

VITAMIN AND MINERAL SUMMARY TABLE

Vitamin	Source	Functions
Vitamin A	Liver, carrots, dark green vegetables, fish, liver oil, eggs, butter, margarine	Vitamin A helps to fight infections. It prevents bacteria and viruses from entering the body by keeping the cell walls strong. It is good for the skin and necessary for vision in dim light.
Vitamin B group, e.g. Thiamine (B1), Riboflavin (B2), Niacin, Folic Acid (B12)	Milk, meat, fish, fruit, vegetables, cereals, eggs, nuts and bread	Helps the breakdown of carbohydrate, protein and fat to release energy. Essential for the functioning of our nerves. The body cannot store the B vitamins for long so a daily supply is important.
Vitamin C	Fresh and frozen fruit and vegetables, products fortified with vitamin C	Vitamin C is needed to fight infections, to help absorb iron from food and for healthy skin. A daily supply is necessary because it cannot be stored by our bodies.
Vitamin D	Produced by the body; also in liver, fish oil, eggs, fortified breakfast cereals, butter and margarine	Vitamin D is formed mainly by the action of sunlight on the skin. It helps the body to absorb and use calcium and phosphorus for strong bones and healthy teeth.
Vitamin E	Many foods, especially vegetable oils, eggs and green leafy vegetables	Vitamin E helps to protect the cells.
Vitamin K	Produced by the body; also in green leafy vegetables, liver	Vitamin K plays a vital role in blood clotting mechanisms.

Mineral	Source	Functions
Calcium	Milk, cheese, fish, beans, sesame seeds, dark green vegetables	Forms the structure of bones and teeth. Because it is in constant demand, a regular supply is vital.
Iron	Meat, liver, dark green vegetables, peas, beans	Needed for the formation of red blood cells which help to transport the necessary oxygen round the body.
Phosphorus	Liver, fish, poultry, eggs, cheese, milk, wholegrain cereals, nuts	Helps build bones and teeth and to regulate many internal activities of the body.

Calcium

Very low calcium levels contribute to osteoporosis. In women, osteoporosis is generally caused by a drop in the level of the hormone oestrogen associated with menopause or ammenorhea (no periods), a low intake of calcium and a sedentary lifestyle.

Salt

Salt is needed by the body, but many people take too much and this can lead to high blood pressure. Salt is lost from the body through sweating but the kidneys increase their retention of salt (sodium) and other electrolytes during exercise so salt loss is low. Adding salt to food is only necessary with intense daily endurance training plus a hot environment plus a low sodium diet.

Zinc, selenium, sodium, potassium, iodine, chlorine, copper, manganese and magnesium are needed in tiny amounts and perform a variety of functions. They are found in a wide range of foods and deficiency is very rare.

Water and Fluids

Drinking adequately is essential for triathletes during training and competition. The sweating and perspiring during exercise leads to huge loss of body fluid. If this fluid is not replaced then dehydration occurs, stressing the body and leading to a decrease in performance and overheating. Water is the most suitable fluid to drink. Serious triathletes in training should drink five litres every day. Drinking is essential before, during and after training sessions. During swimming training particularly, triathletes may not realize that they are losing fluid and becoming dehydrated. Feeling thirsty is not the sign that you should drink: drink often and lots. The colour of your urine is a good indicator of state of hydration; it will be a pale straw colour if you are well hydrated. A loss of as little as 2 per cent of body weight through fluid loss will have a significant effect on performance. Drinking in training will teach you to be comfortable for drinking when racing.

During long races or long training sessions, it may be necessary to use carbohydrate drinks to supply energy to the muscles. It is important that the carbohydrate content of drinks is monitored carefully as too much, although supplying energy to the muscles, will decrease the rate at which water can be assimilated. Water is the first priority and normally the carbohydrate content of drinks should be low.

There is little or no evidence that ergogenic aids improve performance despite the various claims made for bee pollen, caffeine, carnitine, creatine, and so on. However, caffeine is a stimulant and its psychological effects are to increase arousal, attention, motivation and concentration, and some endurance athletes have reported improvements in performance. On the downside, caffeine can have a diuretic effect, causing extra fluid loss. It may also increase the resting metabolic rate which may lead to extra heat production in the body.

Body Weight

One immediate result of starting to train is the loss of weight (almost always body fat). Being both underweight and over weight can have an adverse effect on performance. Even in endurance events like triathlon, athletes carry a higher ratio of muscle than non-athletes and so they may be heavier. Normal body weight charts should be treated with caution. If body fat loss is an aim, one way is to reduce the amount of fat taken in the diet. However, the best advice should be to consult your doctor. Never go on a crash diet as these are likely to be missing essential nutrients. This will undoubtedly affect performance, and indeed, your general health. If you want to lose weight, aim for a gradual weight reduction.

All athletes in training will require more calories than the non-exercising population, but it is important not to eat 'junk' food with high sugar and fat content, and excess calories. Complex carbohydrates include wholemeal bread, cereals, rice, potatoes, pasta, vegetables and fruit.

Other examples of 'good' training food include: wholegrain cereal (muesli, Shredded Wheat, Puffed Wheat, Weetabix, bran flakes, porridge) with low-fat milk and fruit, low-fat milk, fruit juice, whole-

It is important to replenish immediately after an event. © *Nigel Farrow*

meal sandwiches with tuna, chicken, lean meat, cottage cheese, egg, peanut butter, cheddar cheese, Marmite, banana or salad items, baked potatoes and salad, baked beans, spaghetti.

Eating for Racing

For professional triathletes, diet for training and racing is a part of their profession. For most of us, triathlon is just one part of our life. It would be inadvisable to change your normal diet in the days or the evening before a race. You do not need to start eating pasta if you hate it, just because some other people do. Stick with what you know. Generally it is best to avoid

Insufficient water intake leads to a dramatic fall-off in performance. © *Nigel Farrow*

fatty foods and too much protein, avoid food that will upset your stomach (including high fibre food), and avoid too much sugary food or drink.

Whatever you do, be sure to have adequate water.

Be careful not to eat too close to the race. Conversely, make sure that you do eat close enough so that you will not be hungry during the race which will lead to a falling off in performance.

During very long races, your body craves solid food. Bananas, figs and energy bars are recommended because they are easy to digest and will not upset the stomach. Always try eating and drinking in training before using the same food and drink in races. Drink immediately after the swim, and continue to drink throughout the race. Do make sure you are hydrated going into the run by drinking enough on the bike section.

Immediately after the race, drink lots and make sure that you eat some carbohydrate food within 20 minutes if possible. This will aid recovery from the race and will help get you back to training quickly.

PART 4

COMPETITION

CHAPTER 17

MENTAL ATTITUDE

It may be poor anatomy, but it's worth repeating anyway: 'The most important muscle is the mind'.

As sport in general has developed along professional lines more and more in the last twenty years, so it has become more and more important to focus on the extra attributes that will give each triathlete an edge. It is self-evident that athletes of a similar standard will have similar standards of fitness and physical ability. Why then, does one athlete usually beat another although they are both similarly fit? Perhaps it is because that winning athlete believes that she will win. It is a crucial belief and attitude to have: a strong mental attitude. It is important to train mental attitude just as we train physically; we become physically fitter by physical training, therefore we become mentally fitter by mental training.

The importance of mental attitude and sports psychology has become more appreciated in recent times, but it is surprising how few athletes carry out mental training in practice. It is almost as if people believe that sports psychology is important for world class athletes but not for everyday athletes. This is untrue. Perhaps one reason for the lack of enthusiasm is that athletes and coaches feel they do not know as much about mental training as physical training and back away from it. In the physical training required for triathlon, an accepted base is 'train to your weaknesses, race to your strengths'. Similarly if current training of mental attitude is weak, then emphasis should be put on that part of training. Certainly nerves can play a great part in determining how well an athlete will perform in a race, but an understanding of why nervousness becomes greater may well help rather than hinder an athlete.

Sports psychologists talk about 'level of arousal'. In everyday terms, this is dealing with nerves. All athletes will race to their best ability when they are mentally and physically prepared, but some will want to be relaxed before competition while others will need to be tense for a race. Finding that correct level of arousal for each individual is important so each can compete with the best possible attitude.

In many sports, the entry level is for children. For triathlon, largely because it is still a 'new' sport, there are many athletes who have come into it as adults. They have chosen to take part, unlike other sports where children have been encouraged to take part by their parents. This is a very positive point as the sport of triathlon belongs to them and is chosen by them. Training and competing in triathlon has been the athlete's choice and the level of disillusionment and dropping out is likely to be lower. However, there still remains the question of why and how some athletes seem to be able to motivate themselves to be able to maintain pressure when they are extremely tired. It is certainly not just the physical attributes and the training: if it were, then everyone would be able to do it. Knowledge of different types of training methods is shared widely and there are few secrets of training. Yet some athletes always seem to under-achieve while others always seem to over-achieve.

Positive Thoughts

It is absolutely essential that training and racing is approached positively rather than negatively. Negative thoughts will always lead to poor training and poor racing performances. Worrying about racing, wishing that you didn't have to go training or race a particular event, feelings of letting others down by a poor performance – all these will have a negative impact.

The notion of self-belief is very important here. It is not enough to hope or think that you will have a great race, you actually need to believe that you will! That confidence or belief is paramount. It is not only a mental attitude. Negative thoughts produce a different physiological reaction from positive thoughts. Triathletes work less efficiently, become fatigued more quickly and actually train and race with less energy than they would with a positive mental attitude.

Winning Characteristics

It is not only self-belief that is important for success. There are a number of other important qualities required to achieve full potential in training and in racing. Although these may go by slightly different names, they would include:

- self-discipline;
- self-reliance;
- self-motivation;
- determination;
- organization;
- concentration.

Note the importance of 'self' in this list.

Deeper analysis indicates that these qualities can be further divided (see Ogilvie and Tutko *Characteristics of the Successful Athlete*) and that these qualities are necessary in some way to be able to train and race successfully.

Self-motivation and Drive

- A desire to win and to be successful
- A willingness and aspiration to accomplish and overcome difficulties
- Setting high goals and aims

- A positive attitude to competition
- A desire and need to achieve excellence

Aggressiveness

- A belief that it is sometimes necessary to be aggressive in order to succeed
- A willingness to become aggressive and enjoying aspects of confrontation and argument
- Can be forceful to ensure that personal points of view are accepted
- A refusal to be intimidated and dominated
- Will not forget disrespect from others

Determination

- Willing to train hard for a long time, to work on skill aspects until exhausted, and willingness to frequently train alone
- Perseverance in training despite inconsistent results
- Has a long term plan and will persist in training and competition to achieve this

Self-analysis

- Accepts responsibility for actions, blame and criticism whatever the circumstances
- Examines 'when things go wrong'
- Endures physical and mental pain and discomfort, and injury

Leadership and Self-confidence

- Will take control of training sessions and believe that the session is correct and will influence other athletes to conform and join in, often by force of personality; will make decisions and believe them to be correct
- Completely self-confident including the ability to deal with everything that may occur

- Confident in strengths and abilities

Emotional Control

- Emotionally stable and realistic, and not easily upset or put-off
- Will control emotions in training and racing
- Will not allow emotions about negative incidents outside his control

Tenacity and Coachability

- Will accept strong criticism and will not become upset or angry when losing or racing poorly
- Durability, the ability to bounce back from adversity
- Will accept advice and dominant coaching but does not necessarily invite encouragement from coaches although respects coaches and the coaching process and considers good coaching essential
- Accepts and respects team captains, authorities, race organizers and governing bodies

Conscientious

- Follow advice, coaching and training schedules and will consider triathlon and its training as a major part of his life, and will never make excuses

The Success Cycle

Mental preparation is essential for full potential to be used. The success cycle starts with a positive self-image and then the remaining attributes all lead on, one to the other.

- a positive self-image
leads to
- a positive attitude to triathlon
leads to
- having high expectations of yourself
leads to
- better training

leads to
- better lifestyle habits
leads to
- eating and drinking properly and sleeping regularly
leads to
- not taking part in activities which will have an adverse effect on training
leads to
- preparing your equipment immaculately for your race or training session
leads to
- excellent results in training and racing.

These improved mental attitudes and their physical results will almost inevitably bring better training performances and race results. Everything that you have done leads to this and you expect to race well, so you do (a self-fulfilling prophecy). This makes you feel even better about yourself, and ensures that the cycle revolves onwards and upwards.

The success cycle undoubtedly works. However, when things do go wrong, it can be easy to get stuck in the circle of failure. This starts with a negative self-image and proceeds along similar lines of the success cycle, but with all the negatives.

- having low expectations of yourself,
- expecting yourself to do poorly,

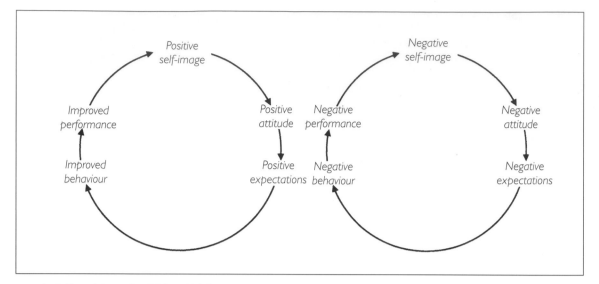

The success cycle (left) and the cycle of failure (right).

- poor training and incorrect lifestyle habits,
- eating and drinking poorly,
- not sleeping enough,
- poor lifestyle habits,
- poor preparing of equipment.

Inevitably a poor race result follows, (once again a self-fulfilling prophecy) and this negative cycle will continue.

There is no doubt that this positive (and negative) cycle works. A positive self-image leads to the other positive factors. It becomes very much a case of being in control and taking control, rather than allowing negative aspects to control you. It is also about feeling good about yourself, and being in control of your life and of your training. It is about the self-belief that *I can* and *I will*. Poor performers are reluctant to take any control, and instead allow other factors to control them.

The positive self-image and positive outlook on life is also a major contributing factor to other examples of a strong mental attitude. Remembering previous excellent race results and previous excellent training sessions will have a huge impact on future racing and training. That 'powerful muscle', the brain, impacts upon and controls muscle responses. The motivation of reliving previous

excellence and visualizing future events establishes a positive pattern, leading once again to that self-fulfilling prophecy. Be aware of dwelling too deeply on poor race results. Rather, decide what went wrong and decide what to do about it in the future. In this way, you are turning negative experiences into positive ones. Our thoughts always influence our reactions, and the anticipation of a pleasant and positive training session or planned race will ensure that reaction occurs. In general, positive thoughts lead to positive reactions while negative thoughts will get negative reactions. Part of mental attitude training should be planned, systematic, conscious and positive thinking. A systematic and positive thought process and analysis can change negative behaviour into positive behaviour.

Positive thoughts can dramatically alter performance while, on the other hand, getting into a pattern of negative thinking will adversely affect performance. Getting into the habit of positive thinking will not happen just by chance; just as physical training builds up over years of repetition, so will mental training. The mind and body both learn from repetition and that repetition takes time.

Some sports psychologists use the **PASS** process.

A positive mental attitude immediately before a race is necessary to race well. Most successful athletes will have a routine (both physical and mental) which they follow before an event. The physical routine may well be their warm-up preparation but they will also have a mental warm-up. Thoughts such as 'I feel calm', 'I want to race', 'I am prepared to work hard', 'I will respond to any situation', 'I fear nobody' will all feature, in some guise. There will be an avoidance of negatives, and a focus on positives.

Visualization

The technique of visualization involves not only seeing yourself doing well in the event, but also bringing in the other senses; what does the race sound like, smell like, feel like? It is important to anticipate these

---

THE PASS PROCESS

Positive thoughts and words
Avoid negatives (*no, never, not*)
Simple thoughts and words
Schedule mental training

Positive mental attitude leads to great racing.
© Nigel Farrow

Assess and think positive! © Nigel Farrow

(especially if it is in a less important race) as athletes can then put into action their prepared plan or coping strategy.

Maintaining a positive attitude, whatever happens, is critical and directly enhances the race performance; without this attitude race performance will be poorer than it should. Setting both short- and long-term specific and dream goals and planning how to achieve these goals is crucial. The visualization and imagination of fulfilling these goals is also essential. This will ensure that preparation and training – both physical and mental – will be successful. The persistence that you bring to training and its repetition is also essential. There are no short-cuts to success: it can be the thoughts about how long it has taken and how much has had to be given up to ensure that success, which will carry you through.

sensations, otherwise they may come as an unexpected shock. It is important to be relaxed but also ready to race and to imagine yourself racing well. Pre-race preparation should include all the positive thoughts of how well you have trained and prepared, how well you anticipate doing, and focusing on your race tactics rather than worrying about any other competitor. Total focus and concentration on the race is essential. Taking a positive attitude into the race and anticipating doing well will ensure that you do race well.

Despite all the planning and positive attitudes, sometimes things do go wrong! It is important then to have a plan, to have coping skills. This should not be confused with negative thinking but predicting and preparing for problems and having a strategy for dealing with them. Dislodged swimming goggles, a puncture or a crash, blisters and sores are all things that can happen and athletes should have a plan for dealing with them. Sometimes when things do go wrong, it can almost be a relief

The final seconds before the race.
© Nigel Farrow

CHAPTER 18

PREPARATION FOR RACING AND COMPETING

Preparation for competition begins with the first training session ever done. For triathletes who intend to compete, rather than the people who use the three disciplines of triathlon to keep fit, competition is the raison d'être of triathlon training. However, there are many triathletes who train hard and efficiently who are unable to compete as well as they train. It is important to examine why this is. Sometimes it can be nervousness approaching a race, perhaps a dislike of competition, sometimes it can be training too hard immediately prior to a race. This can be summed up as **poor pre-race preparation.**

Poor Pre-Race Preparation

In addition to the factors noted above, this can include problems such as having little knowledge of a course, inappropriate kit or equipment, a lack of proper food, lack of sleep, or arriving at a race venue too late. These factors occur immediately before the event. The factor that is often misunderstood and can therefore be misused is the preparation for the race called tapering.

Tapering

Tapering can be difficult to explain and is perhaps the least understood of all the different aspects of training. In short, it can be called the change of training in preparation for a race, and this change is usually to less training. Training is physically chal-lenging and fatiguing; approaching a race and maintaining hard training will mean going into the race tired and unlikely to maximize performance. Training hard leads to tiredness, training less leads to recovery. This is a simplistic view and there are several factors to take into account, but the major purpose of a tapering phase is to allow athletes to recover from the fatigue of hard training before a competition. This requires maintaining the fitness level and minimizing the fatigue level.

Athletes in all sports are often reluctant to reduce the amount of training in the fear that all the hard won fitness and conditioning will be lost in the tapering period. This belief is untrue. Physiological changes and gains through hard training will be maintained even if training is reduced by 50 per cent. It is a so-called 'simmering' effect. Tapering ensures recovery from the hard training. Without the hard training period, the taper period will have little effect. The critical aspects are:

- the quantity, quality and types of training in the hard training period;
- the quantity, quality and types of training in the tapering period.

During the tapering period there will be an increase in glycogen levels because of the extra rest, a maintenance of blood volume levels, a maintenance or increase in muscle strength, and a maintenance in aerobic capacity. However, these will not just occur as if by chance. It is necessary to examine the type and amount of training during that tapering period.

Types of Tapering

Three types of tapering have been widely used in many competitive sports:

- rest-only tapering (ROT)
- low-intensity tapering (LIT)
- high-intensity tapering (HIT).

Rest-only Tapering

This is self-explanatory. For a period of time before the race, the athlete stops training and rests only.

Low-intensity Tapering

Quality training ceases and training is maintained by low-intensity swimming, cycling and running.

In most cases, these two types of tapering do not work. LIT makes little or no difference to a race performance than not tapering at all, while ROT may even reduce race performance.

High-intensity Tapering

This is the best kind of tapering. The amount of time spent training is reduced while the intensity is maintained or increased. The general principles are: less training time, more intensity, more recovery.

The amount of training during the tapering period is less in amount and time but the intensity of the session will be greater. The amount of recovery between the efforts will also be greater. It may be necessary to increase carbohydrate intake although be cautious: it is easy to increase body weight by eating the same amount while exercising and training less. Water intake should be increased. The amount of training should be reduced to between 66 per cent and 50 per cent (or even less). Tapering is crucial for best race performance but is only effective if combined with hard training before the race season.

Progression in high-intensity tapering in swimming

- 6 days before race: 8 × 100m in 90 seconds, 15 seconds rest interval
- 4 days before race: 6 × 100m in 80 seconds, 30 seconds rest interval
- 3 days before race: REST
- 2 days before race: 4 × 100m in 70 seconds, 45 seconds rest interval
- Day before race: 2 × 100m in 60 seconds, 60 seconds rest interval.

If training has not been hard and consistent, there is little point in undertaking a tapering period. Training must be hard for a taper to be efficient.

It is important to do something the day before a race. While it is important to be rested, too much rest will lead to lethargy, a feeling of tiredness. A very short training session, perhaps as little as 10 or 15 minutes on two or three disciplines will ensure that the fast-twitch muscles are prepared.

The same taper does not work for everybody. It is important to experiment before deciding if tapering works, and if so, which type.

Other Tapering and Race Preparation Factors

- When the amount of training is reduced, there are many more hours to fill, particularly before a race. It is easy to sit around with other triathletes and drink and eat more than normal. If you have eaten and

prepared properly then extra, especially junk, food will not help you race better.
- You do not need to taper for unimportant races.
- The individual athlete's reaction to pre-race nerves and anxiety will also determine the exact kind of tapering.
- Mental preparation is at least as important as physical tapering, so do not ignore this aspect.
- Tapering too often loses its efficiency. Early season and unimportant races should be 'raced through' without too drastic a taper.
- Older triathletes may require a longer taper than younger triathletes.
- Too much tapering may lead to a loss of conditioning. Do not taper too often or too much.

Other Race Preparation Factors

Apart from the physical and mental aspects of tapering and preparing for a

race, there are other, less complicated issues to consider.

Food, accommodation, travel and clothing and equipment

Don't make changes to your usual food and diet before a race. There is no perfect pre-race food and changing normal habits may lead to an upset stomach. A good night's rest is ideal but not always possible. Always try to find suitable accommodation.

Give yourself sufficient time to check the race circuit and transition area, particularly the entrances and exits. Ensure that your equipment and clothing are suitable and adequate for the event.

For swimming you will need a wetsuit (if open water) and swimming costume, goggles, and swim hat. For cycling and running you will need a bike and crash-hat, a top to wear for cycle and run, cycle shorts and/or running shorts, cycle shoes and running shoes.

Also remember to take safety pins, puncture repair kit, cycle pump, water bottles and Vaseline.

Checking out transition area stops any silly mistakes. © Nigel Farrow

A quiet place to concentrate can be found anywhere. © *Nigel Farrow*

Remember to have warm clothing for immediately after the event.

Preparation Makes Perfect

Successful racing depends on attention to detail and early preparation. Leaving things late or leaving them to chance will almost guarantee failure. Check your equipment and clothing one week before a race. Particularly check over the mechanics of the bicycle including tyres and tyre pressure (pressure will need to be rechecked later), brakes, gears, handlebars and stem for tightness. Ensure that your travel and accommodation is booked and correct. Maps and emergency contact telephone numbers must be close to hand.

On the day before the event recheck your clothing and equipment, have a water bottle and energy snack by you all the time. Carry the race details with you. Go to the race briefing if there is one. If there isn't, there will almost certainly be a help-desk close to the race registration. Don't be afraid to ask questions, but do make sure that the questions aren't already answered in the race literature. Importantly, ensure that you know your wave start time. Check the event course and routes; drive around the course if it's open to traffic. Ensure that you know entrances and exits to the transition area, including mount and dismount lines for the cycle discipline. Make a note of where the toilets are.

Eat sensibly: don't overeat and stay with food that you are comfortable with. If you are unsure about nearby restaurants, take your own food with you. Try to sleep but if you suffer from pre-race nerves then don't worry, just rest. Be aware that most athletes have disrupted sleep the night before an event.

Check water bottles and all race numbers. Ensure that they are attached where they should be.

Immediate Pre-race Preparation

Many events in Europe start mid-morning or in the afternoon. In Great Britain, early morning starts are the norm. It is important to have adequate time before the event so timetable in extra time in case there are any delays in your schedule. Be prepared for traffic conditions to slow you down and have an idea of where you will park at the race venue. It is important to eat breakfast however nervous you feel. Drink adequately. Water is to be preferred but there is nothing wrong with tea or coffee. Do timetable in more than one visit to the toilets.

Give yourself adequate time to prepare your equipment and any clothing in the transition area. You may have your leg and arm marked with a number before entry

Focus on the swim course. © *Nigel Farrow*

to transition is allowed. It is probable that bike and helmet checks will be carried out as well. Rack your bike and check tyre pressure. The gears on your bike should be set at the appropriate level for starting the cycle section. Finally lay out your clothing, shoes and water bottle.

Mentally prepare for the event; visualize what you will do and then walk through the transition areas, checking the entrances and exits.

Stretching and warming up is an individual choice, but warming up for three different disciplines may not be wise. If possible, do get in the water for a short warm-up. This will give a chance to check your goggles aren't leaking or misting up.

Transition areas and the area near the swim start can be very busy and noisy before the race starts. If you need to be calm and quiet before a race, ensure that you have found a suitable place to mentally prepare.

Get to the swim start early and check that you are in the correct wave start (look for swim hats the same colour as yours). You should already have decided whether you are going to start in the middle of the competitors in the front row, or over to the side or a little further back. This will depend on your swim strength: it's better to be removed from the intense action if you are not a confident, strong swimmer.

Finally, breathe slowly and visualize yourself doing well; tell yourself that if anything goes wrong, you will deal with it immediately and not let it spoil your race. Focus on the swim course.

After the Race

Eat and drink as soon as possible, it will help recovery. Dress in warm clothes. If possible, stretch and have a massage.

World champion Helen Jenkins shows absolute focus pre-race despite being surrounded by her rivals. © Nigel Farrow

CHAPTER 19

ANALYSING PERFORMANCE IN RACING AND TRAINING

Analysing race performance is particularly fascinating in triathlon because there are not only the three disciplines to look at, but also the impact that each of them has on the others. Athletes and their coaches will always want to see where they could have done better and what specific changes they need to make to their training schedules and race tactics to make improvements.

Training Diary

Most athletes in all sports keep training diaries, but how many use them to analyse what worked and what didn't work? A diary will help you work out what sessions were done before a particularly good race, and which sessions before a poor event performance. This is how a training diary should be used, rather than just as a record of distances and times.

Analysis of Performance

Record and analysis of the times in the three individual disciplines are only the starting point in triathlon. For the sake of brevity and clarity, an analysis of an Olympic distance, non-drafting race is used in the example which follows. It could well be a sprint or a long distance event. An analysis of performance is important in order to evaluate and improve performance for future races. It is possible that the athlete can check several of these factors, but in many instances a coach or friend will be needed to record the necessary information.

Swimming

The information to be recorded includes:

*   The overall time you take for the 1500m, from the starting signal to the exit from the water;
*   Assessment of your swim time in comparison to previous races.

The First 100m
It is important to establish a good position in the swim pack.

Drafting is legal in the swim discipline and a significant amount of energy is saved by drafting behind, or very close to, another swimmer. Making a big effort on the start of the race to establish a good pack position is important, even if you overexert yourself to do this; once established in a good position, recovery starts to take place.

The Final 100m
*   Note your ability to get in 'clear' water and make an easy exit into transition rather than be pushing and barging for space.

A significant amount of time can be saved by exiting the water and entering the transition zone alone; there is no need to avoid other athletes and perhaps have to run around somebody, and there is less chance of falling, or being pushed over.

Analysis of race performance is necessary to improve. © Nigel Farrow

> **DRAFTING**
>
> Stay with the pack and save time, become detached and slow down.

- Can you maintain position in the pack of swimmers at the front, or placed in the middle? Remember, drafting in swimming is legal and can have a significant impact on overall swim time and also overall finishing time.
- If you are detached from the pack, how far into the swim did it happen, and why?
- Was too much effort given at the start to join the swim pack? If falling away from the pack after establishing that position, that will probably reflect on a generally weak swim.
- If detached from the pack, note the difference in times between pack/drafting swimming and single swimming. A significantly slower 'single' time will demonstrate poor swimming ability, insufficient training, or possibly, an over-exertion to try to stay with the pack.
- Swim times at each 400m, or at least the first and second halves of the swim. Was there a drop-off in these times or were they similar? A drop-off in times indicates lack of endurance fitness, or possibly poor tactics in starting too fast.
- Overall swim time and position compared to athletes competed against before of a similar standard
- Compare your finishing position and time with athletes against whom you have previously finished very closely.
- Particular local conditions that affected performance: was it very cold or hot, was a wetsuit allowed or not, was there choppy water, windy, strong current or tide? Some athletes are easily affected by adverse conditions, some cope extremely well. The mantra is, 'it's the same for everybody; just do it'.

- Self-analysis: did you feel that you swam well? Was this reflected in your time and position? Were you comfortable in the pack or did you struggle to stay there?

The analysis should reflect your time and position, if not then a more in-depth analysis is required.

Swim to Cycle Transition

This is the information you need for your analysis.

- Time taken in the transition area overall, in comparison with other athletes
- Comparison with athletes raced against previously
- Time taken from arriving at bike and leaving with bike
- Comparison with previous transition times

Cycling

- Overall time for the 40km
- Assessment of cycle time in comparison to previous races
- Split and comparison times for each 5km, or at least the first and second half of the race

Are times comparable throughout the race or slowing down? Slowing indicates poor endurance training or starting too fast.

- Time for first kilometre or 500m

Even in non-drafting races, there is a strong psychological effect of being in sight contact with other, similar standard athletes

- Time for the final kilometre or 500m

It is important to get a clear entry into the transition area, particularly with bikes as there can be the possibility of bikes making contact and athletes falling.

- Cadence on first half of cycle

It is important to select the correct gear ratios. Too big a gear and athletes will tire quickly, too small and there is wasted effort.

- Cadence on second half of cycle

A slowing of cadence indicates a lack of fitness, or choice of incorrect gear ratios.

- Gearing used on first half and gearing used on second half

A necessity to go into a smaller gear may indicate a lack of fitness, or lack of practice on bigger gears.

- Particular local conditions that affected performance: very cold or hot, windy, raining

As with the swim and run, some athletes are easily affected by adverse conditions, some cope extremely well.

- Self-analysis: did you feel that you cycled well? Was this reflected in your time and position? Were you comfortable, were you overtaking or being overtaken or maintaining position after the swim?

- Relative strength of cycle discipline

Cycle to Run Transition

- Time taken in transition area overall in comparison with other athletes
- Comparison with athletes raced against previously
- Time taken from arriving and starting to rack bike and leaving on run
- Comparison with previous transition times

Running

- Overall time for 10km
- Comparison with previous times and races

- Split and comparison times for each 2.5km or at least the first and second 5km

Are times comparable throughout the run or slowing down? Slowing indicates poor endurance training or starting too fast.

- Time for first kilometre

It is important to start the run with good cadence; poor time may indicate lack of training on bike-to-run work.

- Time for final kilometre

If time is very much faster than average of run, this may indicate poor pacing. A slow final kilometre indicates lack of adequate training for the distance.

- Leg cadence; difference between cadence on first and second half of run

Leg speed is the single biggest indicator of running speed and fitness. A drop-off in cadence indicates a lack of fitness, or a lack of training on leg speed, or both.

- Particular local conditions that affected performance: very cold or hot, windy, raining

As noted with the swim and cycle, some athletes are easily affected by adverse conditions, some cope extremely well.

- Self-analysis: did you feel that you ran well? Was this reflected in your time and position? Were you comfortable, were you overtaking or being overtaken or maintaining position after cycle?

- Relative strength of cycle discipline

Overall

- Individual positions in the swim, cycle and run

Were there similar placings/positions in all three disciplines? Or did they vary dramatically? Athletes will normally finish higher when there is not a very weak discipline, even if there is a particularly strong one.

- Comparisons with athletes with whom you are generally similar

As above, compare your finishing position and time with those of athletes against whom you have previously finished very closely.

Analyse everything, including transition. © Nigel Farrow

PART 5

WHERE TO GO FROM HERE

CHAPTER 20

NATIONAL AND INTERNATIONAL STRUCTURE AND ORGANIZATION OF TRIATHLON

World

The world governing body for triathlon, the International Triathlon Union (ITU) (www.triathlon.org) was founded in Avignon, France in 1989 on the occasion of the first official World Championships being held. The official distance for triathlon was set at a 1500m swim, a 40km cycle and a 10km run taking from existing events in each discipline already on the Olympic programme. This standard distance is used for the ITU World Cup series and for the Olympic Games.

Since 1989, the sport has grown rapidly and now has over a hundred affiliated national federations around the world.

In 1994, at the IOC Congress in Paris, France, triathlon was awarded full medal status on the Olympic programme and made its debut at the 2000 Summer Games in Sydney, Australia.

The ITU organizes annual World Championships and the World Cup series.

National

Triathlon in Great Britain is organized by the British Triathlon Federation (BTF) (www.britishtriathlon.org) whose members are the three Home Nations Associations of Triathlon England, Triathlon Scotland and Welsh Triathlon.

British Triathlon is responsible for matters such as the Great Britain Elite and Age Group Teams, British and International events, Anti-Doping and International Representation. British Triathlon also manages a number of services that are shared with the three Home Nations.

Useful Contacts

British Triathlon Federation
Sir John Beckwith Building
Loughborough University
Loughborough, LE11 3TU

Email: info@britishtriathlon.org
Tel: 01509 226161
Fax: 01509 226165
Post: PO Box 25, Loughborough, Leics, LE11 3WX

Triathlon England
www.triathlonengland.org
Tel: 01509 226161
Email: info@triathlonengland.org

Welsh Triathlon
www.welshtriathlon.org.uk
Tel: 01509 226161
Email: info@welshtriathlon.org.uk

Triathlon Scotland
www.tri-scotland.org
Tel: 01875 811344
Email: admin@tri-scotland.org

INDEX